Goal Setting & Morning Routine:

Discover The Blueprint To Achieving Your Goals & Maximizing Your Productivity With Morning Rituals & Success Habits (2 in 1 Bundle)

information is without contract or any type of guarantee assurance.

The trademarks that are used are without any consent, and the publication of the trademark is without permission or backing by the trademark owner. All trademarks and brands within this book are for clarifying purposes only and are the owned by the owners themselves, not affiliated with this document.

Rituals Of The Rich & Famous

Free Success Tips, Strategies and Habits of The Rich & Famous

Four new strategies every week on how to be more productive, confident, and happy.

Join Successful Subscribers!

Morning Routine:

Skyrocket Your Productivity, Enhance Your Energy & Achieve Your Goals With A Fully Optimized Morning Ritual

Contents

Introduction

Mornings are the best way to start living the life of your dreams. Starting the day the right way is truly going to determine the remainder of it. Compounded over time that's going to turn into weeks, months and years of successful living. All just from a morning routine!

Many famous successful people credit their successes to a morning routine.

- Barack Obama
  After around five hours of sleep, Barack Obama wakes up. He drinks either orange juice, tea or water and then exercises before eating breakfast. His exercise routine usually involves either strength training or cardio.

- Oprah Winfrey
  The multi billionaire, media company owner Oprah Winfrey likes to rise early at around 5:30 am. She works out for an hour in the gym and then sips on some fruit or vegetable juice before heading off to work.

- Richard Branson
  The founder of the Virgin Group, Richard Branson likes to sleep with the curtains open so that his body clock is

in sync with the earth's natural circadian rhythm. Upon waking he likes to swim in the ocean, kite surf and play tennis. These habits keep him energized to run his huge empire of businesses.

- Arianna Huffington
  Founder and CEO of The Huffington Post, Arianna Huffington likes to get a long sleep. When she wakes up she practices meditation for at least thirty minutes. This keeps her calm and non reactive which is essential for running a demanding business.

You too can be like them! Start carving out some time in the morning and stick to it consistently. It doesn't have to be an hour long. Anything from five minutes is enough. Just decide that whatever it is you choose to do everyday helps you to achieve your goals and have the best state of mind for your life.

To achieve our best results we need to set aside time, each and every morning. We all have our own unique lifestyles. For some of us the morning might start at different times and feature different activities. That's fine, the most important thing is that you choose to implement a consistent routine that will help and guide your actions. In doing so it will also help you to develop the two fundamental essentials of success, focus and discipline.

Get some small wins and stack them up. If you want to meditate thirty minutes a day then dont expect to start with that much. Begin with five minutes or less and work your way up. The same can be applied to any of the other habits you would like to start. Whether that's reading, exercising or anything else important to you, start small. Keep a track of your success on a calendar or in note form. Just mark an "x" on the day and the time. When you stack up the wins it will motivate you to keep going.

Create triggers that remind you to do the things that matter to you in the morning. For example, if reading is important to you, leave a book next to your bedside. Or if exercise is important to you then lay your exercise clothes out the night before. The easier you make it to happen, the more likely you are to engage in the actions.

If you have stronger reasons behind your morning routines then that will help them to stick. Consider each activity on your routine. List the reasons why it is important to you and become aware of them. That could be things such as reading, to become smarter or learning particular things. Or meditating to become calmer and so on. Knowing why your doing these activities will help you to complete them when the going gets tough and also to feel inspired through doing them. On the days that you struggle, remember that when it's hardest is when you form the strongest beliefs and habits.

Now let us take a look at how to optimize your morning routine. Beginning with getting a good nights sleep.

Sleep

Before you even start your morning routine you need to get the best night's sleep possible. Surveys conclude that over fifty percent of Americans are sleep-deprived or regularly have difficulty falling asleep at night. Our sleep debt is impacting our ability to perform at our best. At night, too many of us waste time watching TV, browsing online or just generally wasting time. We need to understand that sleep is a necessity and not a luxury. That doesn't mean that we need to change our entire lives, instead we just need to add in some quality sleep time.

There is a considerable genetic variation in how easy it is for people to get a good night's sleep. The optimal, average range is around seven and a half to nine hours of sleep. The average sleep cycle is ninety minutes long and the average person has five of those. If you put all that together that's about seven and a half hours.

If you can't find enough time at night then naps can help you. In fact we are the only animal that tries to get all of its sleep in one chunk. Every other animal on the planet is multiphasic which means they break up their sleep times. We used to be that way until the industrial revolution. Even back in Roman times people used to block out time for taking a short sleep.

Your body is equipped with a whole bunch of internal clocks that regulate how and when certain processes take place in the body. They operate over a roughly twenty four hour cycle known as the circadian rhythm. There are external cues that influence how these internal clocks work. These cues include things such as bright lights, food intake, movement and stimulants. You can think of your circadian rhythm as the source code for a software which contains the individual commands that are regulating how the software is working. Any time you input a command into the source code, such as drinking a cup of coffee or exposure to bright light, you're inputting another entry into the source code.Now what your body wants is to have these commands to be as consistent and predictable as possible. That's why it is important to have a consistent sleep schedule.

The first step is to figure out your bedtime. Understand that the amount of sleep we need is roughly around seven and a half hours. In order to get to that we have to be able to schedule our bedtime based on our wake-up time. Wakeup times are determined by work and commitments. Decide on what that is and then stick to it. Once you have your wake up time count backwards from that seven and a half hours.

Everything you do over the course of the day is going to contribute to your quality of sleep in some way either positively or negatively. The first step is to create a really big contrast between the first half of your day and the second part of your day. The bigger this contrast is the more you are going to condition yourself to be relaxed and still when the time for sleep comes.

Daytime is the time to be exposed to a lot of stimulation such as bright lights, social interactions, movement and physical activity. It is the time to get your stressful errands handled, to work hard and get things done. Nighttime on the other hand is the time to let go, to be relaxed, peaceful and just generally wind down.

At night, minimize your exposure to light and in particular blue light because it sends a strong signal to your body that it should be alert and awake. It also suppresses melatonin production which is the hormone that your body produces as you're getting ready to sleep.

Tweak the light bulbs you have at home. You can buy incandescent light bulbs which emit a lower spectrum of light and less of the blue light. Tweak your smartphone and laptop screens to emit less blue light. There are applications which will optimize your devices for this. Alternatively you can buy some blue light blocking glasses which have more orange or red tinted lenses and they will do the job of blocking blue light as well.

During the daytime having lots of blue light is actually a good thing because it's helping to reinforce this big contrast between your daytime and your nighttime. A few things you can do specifically is to get outside as much as possible during the daylight hours. Now for many of us that is only possible to an extent because we are having to spend a lot of time indoors. Particularly if you have an office job. But even going to the nearest balcony every hour or so and spending a few minutes outside is already going to help you.

Besides light, the next thing to be aware of is caffeine. Consider the amount of time for the peak concentration of caffeine in your blood. In the case of caffeine it's about five or six hours which means that you want to space out your caffeine intake sufficiently far enough from your bedtime. Ideally have your last caffeine dose ten hours before bedtime. Substances like chocolate, tea and cocoa powder also contain caffeine so be aware of those too.

Anxiety and stress are another big reason people give for why their sleep is disrupted. Find out how to flip the off switch in your mind so that you're not thinking about things when you should be sleeping. Now flipping that switch is not easy. To help you need to create a buffer zone where you slowly calm down via rituals.

Stress is unavoidable, it is a part of life and some amount of it is actually even beneficial because it helps you to be more alert and productive. High amounts of stress at certain parts of the day is fine. But at night you need very low amounts of it. Therefore you should do the hardest thing first thing in the morning and then progress to easier activities as the day goes on. So for example if you have some stressful issues, deal with all of those early in the day and don't leave it too late. The same applies for socializing. Have easy interactions late on and save the debates for early on.

Avoid distractions like social media a few hours before bed because they can trigger you to be more alert and awake. For example responding to messages or comments. Practice solitude and spending time alone with your thoughts.

Nowadays we are constantly connected. What your brain does when it's just and your thoughts is to try to creatively solve problems and conclusions. The worst time to do all of that is the time when you actually want to fall asleep. So it is important to have dedicated times during the day when you are not listening to a podcast or looking at your phone. It should be just you and your thoughts.

Implement relaxing time into your day by for example, having a couple of commutes where your not doing anything. Or taking a break to sit on a park bench. Or taking an evening walk to reflect and let your brain solve problems. Similar practices that are also effective are journaling or exercising. That could just be stream of consciousness journaling where you literally write your thoughts. Your brain needs to process all the information it receives. Jamming it with social media is filling it up with even more thought loops.

The best way to alleviate stress from any kind of pressing issue is to try to fix the problem and actively do something about it. Don't just hope that the problem goes away. There is a good chance that it won't happen. When you actively try to deal with the stress there is a higher chance that you won't be bothered by it for as long. Exercise and movement in general are excellent for helping with sleep issues. If you can exercise early in the day that might be even better. The only thing to be mindful of here is that you don't want to have a lot of stimulants before.

We also need to make our room a sanctuary cool, dark and mellow. There's an optimal temperature range for sleep.

Cooler temperatures are better for sleeping. Higher body temperatures are associated with wakefulness in your body. Your body temperature is naturally going through fluctuations over the course of the day where it hits a peak at some point during the daylight hours and then it gradually goes down as your sleep time approaches. If your room is very warm that might mess with your sleep. In the winter, that's not a big issue because you can just turn down the heating. In the summer this can be trickier so an AC can help but of course that can be tough on your electricity bill. A cheaper option is to have a ventilator or a fan which is directed towards you.

Then you want your bedroom to be as dark as possible. Our pineal gland and skin are sensitive to light when sleeping so it's very important that it's dark in your room. Ideally you should not even be able to see your hands in front of you. Now this is not that easy to do all the time because maybe you're renting an Airbnb where they don't have blackout curtains. But you can buy some global sticky curtain things or even black bin bag tape up the windows. Add to that an eye mask and your good to go.

Finally, be aware of noise. It;s a good idea to sleep with earplugs in just in case there are any noises during the night. It's super annoying when you finally fall asleep and then some sudden noise wakes you up. If you don't have earplugs then putting in some sort of white noise into your ear helps. You can find a lot of these on YouTube or just download them. Even listening to some sort of speech, podcast or interview can also help during sleeping. If someone is speaking with a very soothing kind of calm tone it just helps you to drift away and fall asleep.

The reality is is that part of living on planet Earth is that sometimes there is value in things that are not completely coinciding with your health optimization quest. For example you might want to go out on a late night date. Or party with friends on the weekend. There can be value to these things and sometimes a thing that might be great for your overall life experience might not be the best thing for your sleep. In general try to get good sleep but every once in a while it might be worth it to do something that goes against that but has more value to you in another area of life.

Snooze Proof Strategy

The alarm goes off and you hit the snooze button for some more minutes in bed. But are those extra minutes in bed actually going to help you? In fact our bodies have chemical mechanisms that will wake us up naturally, without an alarm clock.

Approximately one hour before you wake up the body begins to prepare. Hormones such as cortisol and dopamine are released to give you energy. The problem with an alarm is that it interrupts the natural cycle.

When the alarm goes off your body might not be quite ready to wake up. Oftentimes you will feel groggy and tired, which is a state known as "sleep inertia". The deeper your sleep the stronger the sleep inertia. During this state is when we are more likely to hit the snooze button. But this can do more damage to you than good because when you hit the snooze button your body starts to go back into deeper sleep cycles. Instead of preparing to wake up it is going back to sleep and making things worse.

Here you enter into a vicious cycle. Ultimately it's better not to snooze and if you need to, just set the alarm a bit later. Plus you move your alarm or phone to the other side of the room. Then you will have to get out of bed to turn it off! Try to resist the temptation to snooze and stack up the wins. If you can win the first part of the day your well on your way to success. As the saying goes, if you snooze you lose.

Another thing upon waking that you need to be aware of is checking your phone first thing. Doing this will just put you into a reactive mode all day where your not actually in control of your life. Instead spend some time in the mornings to do your routine.

No checking your emails or social media in the morning. It can distract you and set your mood for the rest of the day. You might come across something negative and then it's going to mess up your day.

Sure there'll be some mornings where you actually have to check something and that's okays. Overall you need to learn to live in the present and enjoy your morning doing what you enjoy the most and doing what sets you up for the day. To help you implement this habit put your phone on airplane mode when sleeping so that when you wake up you won't be distracted by all the notifications.

Intent

Begin each day with a positive intent. That might sound hard to do when Monday morning rolls in too quickly. Your already stressed just thinking about heading to the office and taking care of all the things you need to do. However there is good news because you can make some small changes that will help you to deal with life more effectively and in turn make you a happier person.

Smile

As soon as you wake up, start the day with a smile. Force yourself to smile even if you don't want to because not only does it set a positive intention, it also lowers blood pressure and strengthens your immune system. Start the day right and start it with a smile.

Goals

Keep rolling with a positive intent. Sit up and write out your top goals on a piece of paper. This will bring them into your awareness and again set a positive intent for the day ahead. Always keep a pen and notepad at the side of your bed. Writing by hand will send the goals deeper into your subconscious mind. This is one of the most effective tools to focus your thoughts every day and to set the intention for where you're going to go. It really works, if you think about the color red then all you see is red when you look around the room. Think about your goals and the more opportunities you will see. Planting your goals into your mind when its freshest is the best way to establish them.

Take your goals for the week and phrase them as if they already happened. For example, instead of saying "I set a goal to make $10,000 this week" write out "I made $10,000 this week". Write it out ten or fifteen times in a row on a piece of paper. Do that for two or three areas of your life. You can write down exactly what has happened this week, before if actually even happened. Write down specifically what you want in life as if it has already happened.

I am one of the top sellers in my company
I look and feel ten years younger
I worked out five times this week.
I only fly first class

If you haven't set any goals for your life then this time can be used to figure them out. Write anything you want for thirty days and then analyze the results at the end of the month. Write goals for your health, wealth, career, mind, friends, relationships, travel and adventure. Notice any recurring themes and then those are your goals. Focus on them, break them down and send them into your subconscious mind everyday.

Once you have written your goals it's time to get out of bed!

The Boost

Water

Almost all of your body is composed of water. When you are not taking in water everything in your body is getting dehydrated. After a long nights sleep you will be dehydrated and so in the morning you need to rehydrate right away. Drinking water first thing will hydrate you and speed up your metabolism, especially with cold water. Cold water will boost your body with energy, get the engines rolling and also help to flush out any toxins. Put the coffee down, you can have it later on.

Adding lemon to your water is a great way to boost your immunity. It also contains various healthy minerals and serves as more than enough for your daily recommendation of Vitamin C. This is essential for taking care of vital organs such as the liver. Mix it up with some pink himalayan salt to further boost immunity, improve digestion and balance your body.

This simple cocktail can improve health, vitality and wellness. It will pull the toxins from your cells, giving you better skin and optimal body functioning.

Brush Your Teeth

We all know the benefits of brushing your teeth. Making this a habit of being one of the first things you do is a great way to build your self esteem and respect. Besides that, morning breath can be pretty terrible!

Another benefit to brushing your teeth right away is that it removes any bacteria from your mouth that has accumulated over night. During sleep saliva production which allows bacteria to multiply can eat away at your teeth. Brushing your teeth first thing quickly gets rid of it. Incidentally, this really is the most important time to brush your teeth. Spend time brushing each and every tooth in your mouth. Don't rush through the process, you should take at least two minutes in order to thoroughly clean your teeth. Use mouthwash to rinse off.

Prime Your Mind

The mind is at its freshest in the morning. What you do during this time will have a huge impact on your day. Repeated regularly, it starts to dictate the outcome of your life. Take responsibility and prime your mind for success. A peaceful non reactive mind is one of the best mindstates for us to have. Welcome joy and happiness into your life.

Meditation

Start the day peacefully with meditation and it will carry through your day. In recent times, meditation has become a popular habit. These days there are many applications, courses and classes that teach meditation. It is a powerful practice that can help reduce depression, anxiety and various mental health issues. You don't need to be a monk or a spiritual person to gain the benefits of meditation. It works the same for all of us and it doesn't matter who you are or what you do.

Regular meditation enhances your brain and helps you to deal with stress much more effectively. Not only that but it provides numerous mental health benefits from concentration to calmness and much more. Scientists have also observed that meditation causes your brain to release endorphins. These are the chemicals that make us feel good.

Morning is the best time for meditation because your mind is alert and less prone to distractions. There is less stress at this time of day, especially if you have followed the morning routine and not used your phone yet. If you need more time for meditation, then wake up a little bit earlier. If your too busy then that means you really need it! You will be grateful for all the benefits it provides.

To begin, sit in a comfortable place that is quiet and free from distractions. The best position is to sit cross legged. But if that's uncomfortable for you then you can lie down or sit in a chair. Wear some comfortable clothes and have the right temperature setting. You don't want to be getting up or moving around during your meditation sessions. Some people find value from further blocking out noise and light using eye masks and noise cancelling headphones. These will really allow you to go into a deep meditative state. Try them if you like.

Set a timer on your phone and turn the data off. If your a beginner, start with five minutes and then after some weeks or months of practice, increase the time. The best results come from fifteen to thirty minute sessions. Eyes can be open or closed as you wish. Then you simply breathe in and out. Focus on your breath going in and out of your body. Relax and let your breath flow. Allow your breathing to find its rhythm. Just be.

Stay like this until your alarm goes off. If thoughts enter into your mind, just watch them pass by. If you catch yourself engaging in thoughts then become aware, let them go and come back again to your breathing. If a sound or anything else distracts you let it go and again come back to your breathing.

There are many more styles of mediation. Some involve focusing on breathing whilst others repeat words/mantras and then some even combine meditation with yoga. It's a huge subject and has only been covered briefly here. If your interested to learn more then I suggest checking out some YouTube videos or study a course.

Breathing Exercises

Breathing exercises in the morning can be a great way to wake you up and infuse your body with energy. The most notable breathing exercise right now is The Wim Hof Method. As a result of consistently exposing himself to extreme cold and heat Wim Hof developed the method to withstand such conditions.

To begin get comfortable, you can sit in a crossed legged position or whatever your feel the most comfortable with. Just make sure that your lungs can expand without and restriction. For best results practice when your stomach is empty.

1. Power

Close your eyes. Follow the same style of powerful short bursts of breathing as if you were blowing up a balloon. Inhale through the nose and exhale through the mouth. Maintain a consistent rhythm and allow your stomach to follow. Repeat for around thirty breaths. During this you might feel light headed, don't worry it's normal.

2. Hold

After completing thirty rapid breaths, take in a deep breath to fill the lungs. Let the air out and then at the end hold it for as long as possible. Eventually you will feel the gasp reflex. If you want to, you can add some push ups whilst holding your breath. This will build your strength.

3. Recover

Bring the breath back in to fill your lungs and feel your chest expand. When you are filled with air hold the breath for about ten seconds. This completes one round. Repeat for three rounds in succession.

The three steps process can be repeated in a cycle for around three rounds. After completion take some time to relax and enjoy the feeling.

In addition to The Wim Hoff method or instead of it you can try Tony Robbins breathing technique. This enfuses your body with energy. If you wake up feeling groggy and sluggish try it out. Simple raise and lower your hands above your head as you breath in and out explosively. In through the nose out through the mouth. Repeat for thirty times and do three rounds. In between each round jump lightly up and down and hum for ten to twenty times. Your body will wake up for sure.

Prayer

A short prayer is a beautiful way to focus your time and attention. You don't need to be religious, this could be a prayer to yourself, family, friends or seeking God's advice for the day ahead. Prayer centers us, begins the day with positivity and a focus on your higher self.

Follow the prayers in The Bible or print some out. Personally I have adapted my own over the years. You can do the same. Mine simply gives thanks to my creators, my family god and to wish for health, happiness and success in my goals. Finally I ask for blessings for the people I love and once again give thanks.

"Dear Lord, Farther, Jesus, God.

Thank you for blessing me with this life, family, friends, health, success, love and happiness.
Please guide me to becoming the strongest version of myself today and for the rest of my days. Bless me with love, success, happiness and prosperity in your kingdom.
Please watch over the people I love and help us to live our best lives."

Visualisation

After your prayers a short visualization session will help you to manifest your goals and dreams. That could be for the forthcoming day, week, year or even from your grand vision.

Now there's some big big myths around visualization. First, most people think that when you visualize something it should look exactly like it does in real life. This is where people get demotivated and give up. In fact, it's never like that for anybody.

Instead let me share with you a very simple and highly effective process. First of all, get clear about what your intention is. You need to plant that intention like a seed in the soil of the universe. It will grow as nature will take its course.

Start with the emotion. How will it feel to have the situation, circumstance, person, opportunity or whatever it is you want? How would you behave, how would you sit, stand, walk? Close your eyes and get in touch with the feeling. Out of the feeling images will arise. They might be vague and probably aren't going to look like real life but that's fine, as long as you're connected to the feelings.

The whole process for each goal only needs to be fifteen to thirty seconds at a time. It is not something you need to be pounding the universe with. Because it certainly knows how to respond to your thought energy and emotions. Thoughts create actions. Actions create energy and energy turns into reality.

Affirmations

What if you could somehow brainwash yourself to become successful? Affirmations can help you. They only take a few minutes and can be combined with some physical activity such as walking or yoga. An affirmation is a positive statement that you repeat to yourself which describes how you want to be.

There is a common misconception that affirmations are just like magic pills that make things happen with no effort. This is commonly found in the people who are looking for the easy way or have heard about the power of affirmations. First of all understand that it is action which brings about changes in people's lives. Affirmations are there to help motivate you into taking more action. The more action you begin to take the more the universe is going to work in your favor. Energy responds to like energy and our entire universe is comprised of energy. The more action you take, the more energy you produce. That comes in the form of people, places, circumstances or events that are all designed to help get you closer to your goal.

In order for affirmations to work you need consistency. Affirmations are so easy to forget to do that people end up only doing them sometimes. Also affirmations produce little to no immediate results so people end up giving up because they're not getting the results they want fast enough. Anything worth achieving requires consistency. Affirmations can lead you to your goals so stick with them.

Now the affirmation might not be true but over time it starts to sink into your subconscious which starts to believe it. Essentially you create a self-fulfilling prophecy. Sounds pretty easy right, so then why doesn't it work for some people?

Reason number one is that their affirmations are too unbelievably positive. If I keep telling myself "I am a millionaire, I am a millionaire, I am a millionaire". But your living in grandma's basement eating noodles every night there's a good chance that your conscious brain is going to reject that affirmation. When the conscious rejects it the subconscious rejects it and then it doesn't materialize into your life.

In order for affirmations to work, they first need to be believable to the conscious brain. That way there's little to no resistance. Now it's not that you'll never be able to affirm things like "I'm a millionaire" or something even bigger. What it means is that you need to focus first on making your affirmations small and believable. The more small and believable the affirmations are, the more progress you're going to make. The more progress you make, the more confident you're going to feel in your ability to start asking for bigger and better things.

When it comes time to affirmations your conscious brain is your best friend and it's also your worst enemy. So if you say to yourself something like, "I'm going to be a millionaire" it's going to be like when I'm ninety years old or I'll probably be dead by the time. For that exact reason you want your affirmations to be specific and believable.

Start making affirmations work for you. Forming them in the present tense makes them more believable. Take your goals or mind states that will help you to achieve them. For example:

I am earning 10,000 usd per month online by november this year
I am in a happy relationship by october this year
I am confident and outgoing
I look and feel amazing

Write down your affirmations in a little notebook and carry them with you everywhere that you go. That way you can pull them out and refer to them throughout the day and every morning. It's very very helpful to keep reminding yourself of what it is you're after. This will help you to take more action towards making those dreams come true.

Another thing you can do is to write all of your affirmations on post-it notes and place them all throughout the house or the common areas that you frequent the most. When you wake up, have your subconscious brain absorb those affirmations.

They will really change your life.

Inspiration & Motivation

Instead of starting your day consuming social media or news try feeding your mind with positive information.

Reading

Spend at least ten minutes in the morning reading a book. There's something about reading that really helps your mind with making better decisions. The beautiful thing about doing it each and every day is that you set yourself up to make better decisions throughout the day.

Its well known that some of the most successful entrepreneurs and business leaders are avid readers. Including Mark Zuckerberg, Bill Gates, Mahatma Gandhi, Emma Watson and many more.

Reading has been proven to significantly reduce stress levels, enhance brain power and lower anxiety and depression. Plus all the learning and escapology for your mind. All you need to do is read for a minimum of six minutes per day to start to gain the benefits. In fact, it's often a better alternative to listening to music or going for a walk. Plus if you read for upto thirty minutes a day you can even start to add years to your life!

The most successful and wealthy people prefer educational material and tend to read non fiction books. Biographies of successful people are particularly popular with them. However many also enjoy fiction, particularly at night because it helps them to unwind and sleep. In addition reading fiction has the power to increase emotional intelligence. In conclusion reading can significantly change your life for the better, so make it a habit and part of your mornings.

Quotes

If reading a book is a bit too much try reading some simple quotes. You can find literally millions of quotes online. Quotes will lift your spirits and motivate you for the day ahead. Go ahead and find some online, print them off or write them down somewhere you can look at every morning.

Gratitude

Gratitude is a simple way to bring to your attention the things in your life that mean something to you. With such a strong emotion in your heart, it's harder to fall into negative thinking. Bring gratitude into your awareness every morning with gratitude journaling.

The premise gratitude journaling is to list out several different things that you are grateful for. Be as detailed as possible with whatever it is that you're grateful for. By doing this you are shifting your thoughts into positive directions. When you are aware of all that you have instead of being focused on the have-nots. Focus on the good, especially when you are going through difficult times. Later you can flip back to any given day and read what it is you are grateful for.

Gratitude journaling takes just a few minutes to do in the morning. Try the five minute journal out. Simply record three to five things your grateful for each day. Reflect on your life and count your blessings.

Journal

Another tool you can use to change your life is journaling. This is a cool way that you can coach yourself. You can go back to get insights so you don't lose them and continue to evolve.

There are a number of ways you can journal. Once of the most beneficial and easiest to follow is stream of consciousness journaling. As the name relays it means literally writing down your thoughts without censoring them. Put pen to paper and don't stop writing. You can either set a timer for five minutes or more. Alternatively you can set a page count, say three pages and then stop. That's all there is to it. No editing or going back. Just put down on paper whatever is on your mind.

The purpose of journaling is to free up your mind so there is nothing weighing it down for the day ahead. This method has been proven to help with depression and to organize thoughts. Oftentimes we get stuck in a circle of negative thoughts or something is bothering us at the back of our minds. Putting it down on paper releases you from it. In addition when we sleep our brain resolves things we went to sleep thinking about. Journaling in the morning will help to bring more clarity to any ongoing issues you have.

Have no filter when you write. You don't need to look back on it. Essentially its therapy for your mind. You can even be negative and complain here if you like. Get it all off your chest. It's better than putting that out into the world in the form of gossip or complaining. Just make sure no one ever reads it! Put your most honest thoughts on there. Even your darkest secrets, fears, fantasies or negative thoughts. You might find that you don't necessarily agree with them. Eckart tolle is often quoted as saying we are not our thoughts. This process will help you to see what is real and what is bs in your mind. Unblock your mind with journaling.

If you want to start journaling in the morning then set aside the time to do it. Journaling should take from ten to forty minutes. The more the better. But of course we all have a finite amount of time. The time you spend on journaling will pay off though so maybe get up a bit earlier to do it.

Make sure you use a pen and paper since it is much more effective and you should avoid any screens during the first hours of your day. There are many applications and word processors that can help you to digitally capture your notes. Speed isn't something you should be concerned with here. Even if your writing sucks just take more time on it. When you write longhand it catches more of your thoughts. It also keeps a fresh mental break from the digital world.

Mobility

After sleeping for a good seven to nine hours your body will be quite stiff and in need of some stretching. Yoga and Tai Chi are both great ways to start moving your body. Once you start practicing them regularly in the morning, your body will become accustomed to waking up much more easily. Which means you will feel more awake and energized.

Yoga

Yoga is a very easy exercise to learn. Long term practice helps to maintain a healthy body and mind. You don't need to take a full class to get the benefits. Ten minutes or more is plenty. Even on the days where you feel tired and groggy simply doing some basic yoga will put you into the right state of mind.

The practice of morning yoga will warm up your body helping the blood and nutrients to flow through it. This helps to alleviate aches, pains and promote a better posture. All of which strengthen your immune system for better health and mobility. Combined with a focus on breathing it stimulates your body and wakes up your brain. It's almost like having a fresh cup of coffee but without the side effects!

If you work at a desk or sit for long hours during the day then your body craves the stretching that yoga offers. It will set your body up for a better strength during the day.

You can learn some basic Yoga on YouTube. Load a video and follow along. Learn some basic poses and then everyday, practice the ones that suit you the best.

Tai Chi

If yoga doesn't fit with you then Tai Chi can be a great alternative. Or you could even practice some martial arts drills from Muay Thai, Jiu Jitsu and so on.

Tai Chi is a traditional Chinese exercise that is based in martial arts and involves slow movements combined with deep breathing. Learning it is quite easy. As we have discussed movement and breathing promote various health benefits. Both physical and emotional. Reducing stress and anxiety is one of the biggest benefits of Tai Chi. Numerous studies have concluded this fact. Since Tai Chi also incorporates a form of meditation with exercise it has a great advantage. All this will help to improve your mood, health and sleep whilst alleviating negativity and ill health.

Tai Chi is accessible to all ages. When your starting out you may experience some aches and pains but after more practice those will go away to make you become stronger. As you progress, pay attention to proper posture and precision. It might help to study on Youtube, get an instructor or take a few classes to learn the basics. There are a few different styles of Tai Chi so experiment with them and try the one that feels right for you.

Both Tai Chi and yoga involve meditation and movement. Therefore they have similar benefits and are an excellent addition to your morning routine. All you need is ten minutes a day. Start practicing one of them every morning and celebrate your improved health and happiness.

Exercise

Besides yoga and Tai Chi there are a number of other ways you can work out in the morning. The two most popular are of course weightlifting and running. Health experts recommend mixing aerobic (running/cardio) with anaerobic (weightlifting/strength training). Aerobic exercise uses oxygen on a steady supply whilst anaerobic uses more short bursts. You can choose either or both for your morning.

Weight Lifting/Strength Training

The best time to hit the gym is first thing in the day. This gets it done and out of the way. It also sets a positive tone for the day by breaking through early resistance.

When you wake up hormone levels, particularly testosterone are at their peak. These help you build muscle mass much quicker. Taking advantage of high levels is a great way to get ripped and muscular. Working out early on will also boost your metabolism which plays a vital role in burning fat. This allows your body to burn more calories, even when your not exercising.

Get your workout in early in the day. You will be more free from distractions and the crowds will be smaller. After work it will be much harder to summon the willpower to go. So do it while you can and whilst your body is best wired for it. Then you can go on and enjoy your day including quality time with your loved ones.

But it's not always going to be easy to motivate yourself. So here are some tips to help you go to the gym, first thing. Prepare your clothes and everything you will need the night before. Pack all your gym clothes, protein, towel and anything else you might need. This will lower the resistance to going. Plus the decision has already been made in your mind.

Make sure you keep working on your motivation to hit the gym. That might be a goal to reach a certain weight, look a certain way or feel better. It could even be avoiding going to the gym when it's busy. Sometimes all you need to do is just show up.

Morning Run

Getting out of bed in the morning is hard enough, let alone trying to go for a run! However there are a number of great benefits to a morning run and you don't need to be an Olympic athlete to reap the rewards of morning running. More energy, focus, better sleep and weight loss being some of the biggest benefits. Plus you will feel great that you have already worked out before the demands of the day starts.

When you begin a regular routine of running in the morning your body clock will start to adjust and you will wake up easier. At the start it's going to be hard and you will feel sluggish. But go ahead and persevere!

There are some great tricks you can use to help you start running in the morning. Spike your sugar and energy levels with a banana before running. Or drink a cup of tea or coffee to give you that boost for the run. Have your running shoes and clothes laid out the night before so there are fewer barriers between you and getting on with the run. Do a short stretching session to warm up your muscles and put you in the right mood. When you begin the run you can start slowly. Eventually you will begin to wake up and pick up the pace. Keep a record of your runs and have some goals to reach. Listen to some music whilst you run and get inspired.

Freshen Up

After some good stretching and exercise you will have worked up a little sweat. Also during night your likely to sweat. A good shower is not only cleaning and cleansing, it also improve various bodily functions.

These days there is a lot of debate as to the benefits of hot showers versus cold showers.

Hot Showers

Hot showers can help to rejuvenate muscles. If your regularly lifting heavy weights then a hot shower could be a good idea for you. They also improve blood circulation which will help to ease pain and reduce inflammation. In addition if your suffering from a case of the flu or a blocked nose then a hot shower can help to unblock your sinuses. Furthermore pores in the skin are softened and unclogged with the steam from a hot shower. This leaves a much cleaner and smoother skin surface.

Cold Showers

Cold showers are a bit daunting first thing in the morning but there are a number of benefits to them. Psychologically they are going to build willpower. Overcoming the fear to jump into that cold shower will help you considerably when you face challenges in your life. Then there are the health benefits. Cold water helps to close the pores of your skin which makes it much more firm and appear youthful. It also makes hair stronger. Immunity and blood circulation are also improved as a result of cold showering. This can help to speed up recovery.

Now after all that you might be confused as to what temperature to set your shower! The best way is to choose a temperature that feels the most beneficial to you. However there are times when one can be more beneficial than the other. If you suffer from insomnia a hot shower will adjust your body for a better sleep. If you are prone to acne then cold showers will be better since they close skin pores. If you suffer from cramps then a warm shower will help your muscles to relax. In addition, you can also alternate between cold and hot showers to improve blood circulation and detox your body.

Questions

Your level of happiness and fulfilment is not based on your circumstances but instead on how you perceive your circumstances through your own mental and emotional filters.

These filters are shaped by various factors including, culture, upbringing, religion, experiences and values. Who you believe you are and your story of yourself are influenced by these factors.

We can begin to change our habits and perceptions for the better by rewriting these filters. The most effective way to do that is by asking ourselves better questions. When you begin to consistently ask better questions your perception of your circumstances will change.

Instead of focusing on what you lack or what you want from someone focus on what you can give or what makes you happy. Encourage yourself to find ways to overcome obstacles and plateaus in your life. Identify where you can improve and how. Questions can help you with all of this and much more. Raise the quality of your life with quality questions.

When taking a shower its a great time to ask some questions that will enhance your state and focus your attention on the things that matter the most to you. Questions stimulate thought and motivate you. Here are some questions you can ask and answer out loud to yourself.

- *What am I grateful for? How does that make me feel?*
- *What am I proud of? How does that make me feel?*

- *How can I add more value to the world today?*
- *Who do I love? Who loves me?*
- *What is a decision I can make that would remove a hundred other decisions?*
- *What if I did the opposite for today?*
- *What is the worst that could happen? Could I get back from there?*
- *If I could only work 2 hours per week on my business what would I do?*
- *What would this look like if it were easy?*

__Breakfast__

Many people believe that breakfast is the most important meal of the day. But did you know that you can lose fat and increase muscle mass with fasting?

The most popular fasting method right now is intermittent fasting which typically involves eating all of your meals during an eight hour window. For the other sixteen hours you don't eat anything. It's actually pretty easy to incorporate into your life since for eight hours your asleep anyway. That usually means skipping breakfast and late night meals. For example if your last meal is at 8pm, you sleep at midnight and wake up at 8 am. In that case your first meal would be at 12pm. Each of our schedules are going to be different so you can adjust those times to suit yours.

Intermittent fasting is not a diet, it's a way of scheduling your eating so that you get the most benefits. Which is a great way for you to become more lean without having to worry about what you eat. Whenever your body is full and in a fed state it is very hard to burn fat. Normally your body takes three to five hours to absorb and digest food. After that time you enter into a fasted state where insulin levels are much lower which makes it easier for your body to burn fat.

Diets long term are more difficult to stick to because they soon become tedious based on the limitation of only certain foods. Intermittent fasting, on the other hand can quickly become an easy lifestyle change to implement since it only requires thinking about consuming food within a set time period.

Losing fat is just one of the main benefits of intermittent fasting. It also makes your day much more simple to plan. Not only that but you save time in the morning since you don't have to worry about breakfast. Studies have even found that intermittent fasting can lead to longer lifespans. In particular, a lot of research has studied the relationship between cancer and fasting. Patients showed signs of reduction in cancer when fasting.

There are a few different ways to go with intermittent fasting. You can try one day of normal eating, no time restrictions and then the next day a full twenty four hour fast. Or you can go with the first method explained, eat for eight hours and fast for sixteen hours.

The mental barrier is the main obstacle to people trying fasting because in reality it's not that hard. You might be concerned about skipping breakfast and maybe you love breakfast foods. So just delay them.

You can learn more about intermittent fasting by reading and watching materials, but the best way to learn is to experiment.

Eating Breakfast

If your still concerned about your weight but don't want to try intermittent fasting then eat a healthy breakfast instead. Eating breakfast can be good too because it breaks the nighttime fast and kick-starts your metabolism.

A healthy breakfast should contain nutrition, fill you up and provide enough energy for the day ahead. Here are some of the best foods to get you going.

Oatmeal

Oatmeal is loaded with nutrition and keeps you feeling full for hours. Oats contain powerful antioxidants, protein and fiber. These are great for building a strong body and providing lots of energy. Add in some fruits and almond milk. A great way to begin the day.

Eggs

Eggs are a popular breakfast choice. They are clean, nutritious and full of protein. If you're counting your carbs then eggs are a great choice. Serve them scrambled, poached, fried or boiled.

Nuts & nut butter

If you are vegan or vegetarian then eating nuts is a great alternative source of protein and natural healthy fats. Nuts are also rich in antioxidants which can help you live longer if consumed regularly. Serve some nut butter on your toast or mix them in with some fruits.

Coffee

A cup of coffee in the morning is another popular breakfast choice because it gives you a kick start. If your doing intermittent fasting coffee can also help to stave off hunger in the mornings. Choose decaffeinated coffee and you decrease any health risks. Also avoid adding any cream or sugar. Americanos and espressos all the way.

Tea

If your not into coffee but still need a little bit more energy in the mornings than tea can help you. Tea also contains many powerful antioxidants which support your immune system and promote long term health.

Fruits

All kinds of fruits are an excellent start to the morning. Most are low in calories and jam packed full of valuable nutrients and vitamins which help fight diseases. Add them to your cereal, oatmeal, yoghurt or eat them on their own. You could even blend them as a smoothie.

Flaxseed

Flaxseeds can be sprinkled onto your yoghurt, oatmeal or cereal. They protein, fiber and omega 3. This can help to lower cholesterol and improve blood sugar levels. Make sure to grind the seeds down so they can pass through the body without breaking down.

Cereal

There are millions of cereals out there. Just choose one that has some great nutritional content and you're good to go. Avoid anything that is too processed or loaded with chemicals and sugars. Sugars will spike your energy but leave you crashing later on.

Greek yogurt

Greek yogurt is a great source of protein. It also contains calcium and probiotics which support a healthy gut and immune system.

Cottage cheese

If you're looking for another source of protein than cottage cheese is loaded with it. It can also stave off hunger for longer. You can eat it by itself or it goes well with peppers, dried fruits and nuts.

Vitamins

Get some vitamins into your body first thing to set your engines rolling. There are millions of vitamins out there. Choose the ones that you think will add value to your life. Also make sure to choose high quality ones from trusted companies. Check the reviews. Here are some of the best.

Protein

Besides being great for building muscle a protein shake in the morning is a convenient and healthy option. Even better if your travelling since you won't have to worry about having to find decent food or spending too much money on breakfast.

Mix up some protein with milk, water or even almond milk. Give your digestion a rest and supplement it for food as being a liquid breakfast. Choose protein powders that are low in sugar and preferably dairy free.

Gingko

Ginkgo (Ginkgo biloba) is an extract taken from the leaves of one of the oldest living tree species. They help to improve blood circulation due to their powerful antioxidant qualities. Also it has often been associated with improving memory. They can be taken in tablet, capsule forms or even drank in tea.

Spirulina

Spirulina is a microalgae with lots of nutritional value and health benefits. According to the National Institutes of Health (NIH) Spirulina is promoted as helping with various health issues including weight loss, heart health, diabetes, mental and general wellbeing. Combined with zinc it can help cleanse the body. Can be taken in powder diluted with water or capsule.

Apple cider vinegar

Apple cider vinegar has been around for centuries. Weight loss, improved circulation, immune healing and digestion are just a few of its claimed health benefits. Mix one to two tablespoons with water every morning before you eat anything.

Turmeric

Turmeric is another supplement that can be taken to help with improving digestion and inflammation. Inflammation is one of the biggest issues people have when it comes to their health. Mix about a teaspoon of turmeric with water and it is more than enough.

Gelatin/Collagen hydrolysate

This is good for your joints specifically connective tissue repair to make sure you don't have any injuries and recover quicker. Protect your joints before it's too late. One to two tablespoons of this will serve you well.

Fiber

Fiber is a really important part of your diet. Fiber helps to improve digestion which is a massive part of how your body functions. There are various capsules or even chewy tablets available. Go with the ones which digest the easiest.

Multivitamins

There's a lot of debate out there about whether or not multivitamins vitamins are worth taking because a lot of people think that you don't absorb them. The best way to tell is to experiment with different ones. Check reviews and also observe if your urine is looking any different when you take them. If it does look different than usually that's because your urinating the vitamins out and the body is not absorbing them. Find ones that don't just flush out of your body.

A good multivitamin should contain all the important vitamins. Including Vitamin A for immune function. Vitamin B for health and energy. Vitamin C for preventing and treating colds and Vitamin D for strong bones.

Omega-3 fish oils

Omega-3 fish oil are loaded with docosahexaenoic acid (DHA) and eicosapentaenoic acid (EPA). These are important and beneficial for overall heart health. They also help to lower blood pressure and reduce heart diseases or attacks which are extremely common these days. Everyone should eat fish at least twice a week because they are high in omega-3 fatty acids. For those who do not like eating fish Omega-3 fish oils are a great alternative.

Tribulus

Another natural supplement. This one is for the men because it helps with boosting testosterone, libido and stamina. Research has concluded that men's sexual desire increased by over seventy percent after consuming Tribulus for two months. Take one to two capsules a day.

Creatine

Creatine is a supplement which helps to improve strength and performance in the gym. Various studies have concluded that it can increase muscle size, strength and exercise performance. In addition it helps to protect against neurological disease.

Probiotic

The bacteria levels in your gut play a huge role in your immune system and your body's ability to process infections and bacterias. Probiotics are really important in helping with gut health. The brain of your body.

Echinacea

This is another supplement to boost your immune system. Widely used to stave off infections and colds. Can even be used on the skin to treat wounds or infections. Available in many forms including tablets, juice, and tea.

Whilst You Eat

Whilst you eat and get dressed put on a podcast, music, audio book or some inspirational talks. Fill your mind with goodness.

Podcasts, talks and audiobooks

Here are some of my favourites.

- Impact Theory
- Sadhguru
- Eckhart Tolle
- Joe Rogan
- Success Habits
- Joel Osteen
- Elliot Hulse
- Ted Talks
- Naval
- London Real

- [Jordan Peterson](#)
- [Tai Lopez](#)

Music

If your not a big fan of talks and audiobooks then put on your favourite songs. I have a playlist for the mornings when I really need some motivation. I like to put my favourite uplifting songs here. Nothing sad or dark. Only songs that put a smile on your face and make you want to sing and dance along. Even if you can't sing or dance, do it! It will put you in a great mood for the day ahead.

<u>Most Important Task Of The Day</u>

Showered, dressed and ready to take on the world! By now you should not have checked any emails of social media. You are in control of your day and not in reaction.

Now is the time to tackle your most important task of the day. This is the task or activity that will create the most significant results in your life. That could be planning the day, a business task that gives the most results or even going to the gym. Whatever is the most important thing in your life, take care of it first. Ideally it should be something that requires a significant mental focus since your brain will be in an optimal state at this point of the day.

Focus on what produces results. Not all of the activities and tasks in your life are equal. Some hold more weight than others and thus contribute to more value. You should be continuously aware of what are the most important things in your life. Personally I like to do weekly reviews of all my goals, actions and areas of my life. I can then begin to prioritize the things that matter the most. Pay attention and don't get caught up in going through the motions.

All it takes is a few minutes each day to identify the tasks which are the most important. You can then designate the time and amount of time to work on them. Then you can work your way down the priorities and any things that come up along the way. In time you will be equipped to deal with challenges and priorities.

After your morning routine create a list of the most important tasks. This could come from a master list that you set up on the weekend. Then focus on getting these done. They could be recurring activities as well. Even better if they are because it will reinforce the habit. Ask yourself, what are the most important things that I need to do today? How would they make a difference? Combine this with setting a deadline for the tasks to be done by. This will help you to complete them much quicker than you imagined. Structure your day to make sure the most important tasks are done first and then your on your way to more success.

Plan Your Day

Planning your day makes a massive difference to achieving your goals. It cuts out time wasted and allows you to focus on the activities, people and things that matter the most to you. Instead of being busy being busy and never really achieving anything plan the day before it starts and your productivity will be much higher. Ideally you should plan the night before so your mind is ready when you wake up and has more reasons to get up. But you can also do it in the morning. As you wish!

The first step to planning your day is to understand how much time you have available and when it is available. When your planning the day you need to work around the regular activities in your life such as going to work, events and so on.

Make a list of all the things you need to do. Don't stress or worry about it just let your mind release all of it. Include everything from picking up your laundry to cleaning the bathroom, working on your business, going to the gym and yeah you get it.

Prioritize your tasks and set a time for them. Decide how long they will take. Everything on any list should be assigned a time and priority. Schedule time for your, goals and projects.

Determine the outlook of your day and any open time slots for things to fit in. Most things will be recurring like going to the gym in the morning, then going to work and so on. That can come from your week plan. The day plan is where you focus in on each hour of the day. Make sure you put time in there to buffer where you get to relax or spend quality time with friends and family. Put in any activities and appointments for the day also. Its best to work in one hour time slots here.

Make use of your calendar for upcoming events and things you need to be reminded of. Be sure to check this everyday and set up reminders for the important things.

Having this plan in place doesn't mean you have to rigidly stick to it. Of course things come up during the day and we need to take care of them as they do. But by having some basic planning in place your time will be spent much more wisely leaving you fullfilled and happier.

Conclusion

Morning routines!

Now you have all you need to know to set up a good morning routine. Everything outlined in this book serves to guide you. Ultimately the best morning routine is the one that feels right for you. Choose what resonates and benefits you. What works for me might not suit you and vice versa. With your whole morning routine you want to only use the activities that benefit you the most. Maybe you can drop some that don't add value to you and extend times of others that do.

Design your own based on your needs and the kind of person you want to be. If time is tight but you need to reduce stress then just do some meditation or journaling. Or if your health conscious skip breakfast and do some Tai Chi. Over time you can review what works for you or what you might need to add. The choice is yours.

Take note of the activities you do. Take note of the times you don't do them. Track all of it, including those times when you snooze or miss something. When you start to see the wins stack up is when your habits start to form stronger. Winning early on is one step further to reaching your goals.

Start tomorrow morning and make it your morning routine a habit. You will see how much your life improves from it. The simple application of discipline to do a morning routine will give you massive confidence and self empowerment.

As each day passes you move closer to your goals and becoming the best version of yourself.

I wish you all the best!

Oscar Monfort

Goal Setting Success:

The Blueprint To Setting Goals & Achieving Them

Contents

INTRODUCTION

Stefani Germanotta was born in New York, on March 28, 1986. From the age of four she began playing the piano. By fourteen years old she had written her first piano music and performed in a New York nightclub. A few years later she was just one of twenty students in the world to be granted early admission to the prestigious New York University's Tisch School of the Arts. Whilst there, she continued to elevate her songwriting skills and music. Funding her studies was not easy and to make ends meet, she took on various jobs. One of which included working as a gogo dancer where she learned about burlesque.

Fast forward to 2005 and she was briefly signed by the legendary Def Jam Records. However just a few months later she was dropped by the label. Being dropped motivated her to perform and refine her burlesque performances in venues around New York City. There she also collaborated with rock bands, and began her experimentation with other musical styles. In 2007 she began working as a songwriter at Interscope Records for other artists on the label, including Britney Spears and The Pussycat Dolls. After seeing her perform a burlesque show the R&B singer Akon signed her to his label to start recording her debut album, The Fame. The album received positive reviews and was a massive international success.

Lady Gaga knew she was a star way before the rest of the world did. She would repeat this to herself everyday saying. "'Music is my life and I'm going to make a number-one record,'" One day it became true, many times over. Until now she has had more than four number one albums plus countless top ten hits. Goal setting played a huge part in her success.

Goal setting is powerful.

It is about taking steps towards a future that you want. Do you ever feel like life just happens to you and it's out of your control? Maybe when something good happens you attribute it to good luck. Maybe you have a rough idea of what you want but you're not really sure how to get it. Well the answer to your curiosity can be found in goal setting. So often we don't live upto our full potential because we procrastinate.

Naturally we assume that we can do it at some point and that doesn't have to be now. But before you know it time passes you by. The years fly by. A year feels like a day. But a day should feel like a year. Life should be full. To become a success you will need to have some goals set. But the problem is that too many people are drifting through life. When you don't set goals then you're never going to live up to your full potential. Maybe you're working really hard but not getting anywhere worthwhile. This is because you're not spending time to think about what it is that you really want from life. Without setting specific objectives you end up going nowhere. Think about it like this, would you try to drive somewhere without a map or GPS? Goals are the destination and setting them is the map. A life without goals has no direction and is aimless. When you know your life purpose and turn your dreams into achievable goals and then act on them, you're guaranteed success.

My name is Oscar Montfort and I used to drift through life. With no clear goals I took what life gave me. Which was not always what I expected. Jaded and frustrated I found answers in goal setting. I successfully quit my job last year and have since seen my income grow and my hours shrink. Not only that but my health is excellent, I have great relationships and spend my time doing what I love. Goal setting gave me this blessed life. It gave me something to aim for. When you have a clear destination it heightens your awareness of how to get there. No doubt, challenges will come along the way but your mind will stay focused on your goal. That journey starts with the question. What do you really want in life? The answers to that question will present you with a path.

With a clear vision for your life it will focus your efforts to achieve what you want. Your mind is clear of the things that stress you out and focused on what matters. Goal setting allows you to set boundaries and push the distractions away. Setting goals that matter to you manifests those things into your life. In effect your life will be changed for the better. The difference between a successful person and one who is not is that most people are unsuccessful because they didn't define their goals in the first place. To be a winner, you need to define your goals and go to work on them.

Time is the great equalizer of rich and poor. It is your most valuable asset. When it is gone it can never be recovered. When you have goals your time can be managed much more effectively so that you don't have to waste precious time on things that may never benefit you. Goal setting allows you to allocate enough time for the things of most importance. Ultimately you are shaping your future. Goals help you to shape the destiny you wish for. The moment you set them, they become a plan for the future. No more wandering aimlessly in life, take control of your future. This gives us hope for the future. When you have hope it gives you motivation to work towards achieving it.

The truth is that achieving your goals is a journey. A journey that should be worthy and enjoyable. You need to enjoy it. There will be times where your motivation slides up and down over time. Goal setting is not just saying you want something to happen and wishing for it. You need to clearly define what you want and why. This book will show you how. We are all capable of achieving goals beyond our personal expectations. Believe me I'm proof of that. With goal setting you can raise the bar of your potential and push yourself to achieve things that before you only hoped was possible. Now if you don't already set goals then let this book show you how to begin. As you make goal setting a part of your life, you'll find your life accelerating.

Let's begin.

WHAT IS GOAL SETTING?

Goal setting is essentially about choosing a specific objective that you want to achieve within a specified time. Simply put, goal setting is the act of selecting a target that you want to achieve and through this we can measure ourselves. Success in life, work, relationships, health and everything else in between requires goal setting. When we have goals it gives our life purpose and something to strive for.

Understand that goals can be applied to any area of your life. They can include personal, health, business, romantic, spiritual, career and more. Those can be long or short term. The choice is yours and I'll show you how to make your goals happen. Setting the right goals with the right plans is going to give you the success that you want from life. Goals will give you focus, direction and motivation to wake up everyday and go after your life. They will keep you away from the stupid stuff and ultimately will determine if you're going to be successful.

Now setting a goal is easy because after all who doesn't want to make loads of money? Or have an amazing body? Or a relationship with the person of their dreams? The real challenge isn't setting the goal, it's about asking yourself are you willing to accept the sacrifices required to achieve that goal? Because going for a goal is going to require some sacrifices to achieve it. It's not all going to be glamorous and fun. For example olympic athletes who set goals to win a gold medal. Sure that's an amazing goal to go for. But behind achieving those few seconds of glory are years and years of struggle, discipline, dedication and hard work. Are you willing to do what it takes to achieve your goals?

Now it doesn't matter what age you are or what your circumstances are. Goal setting is about changing those circumstances and making your life better. Goals not only affect behaviour but they also affect your performance. It's proven that they give you more energy which will lead to a higher effort and this will increase the results in your life. When we are sufficiently challenged it helps to motivate and encourage us to perform at a higher level which in turn leads to a higher level of success. A well set goal will require you to make significant efforts. This is really important and beneficial because it will stretch your capabilities and grow you as a person. On your journey towards your goals you're going to meet many obstacles. Overcoming those obstacles will require persistence. Some goals may also require you to change and develop certain behaviours.

Goal setting focuses you on the actions and behaviours that you need to implement to achieve your goals. For example if you have a goal to save a certain amount of money it's going to influence you to be more smart with your money. To make better financial decisions. That's a step in the right direction and will give you the kind of life you want and cut out the stuff that you don't want. Just think of the colour red and you will see the colour red around you. Or for example if you set the goal to meet an attractive new partner then that's going to be more in your awareness. It will influence more of the right activities and actions towards achieving that. Once you start taking the right activities and actions you will build momentum. Just like a snowball gets bigger when it rolls down the mountain this will be the similar effect of you going towards your goals you become better and more effective.

Finally goals will build your character to become a more actualized person. Self mastery is a critical component of setting goals. It's about becoming the best version of yourself. Goal setting will help you to do that and much more.

Goal setting requires some essential skills in order to be successful. These are skills that can be learnt and developed through practice. Those will be discussed in more detail later on but for now let's take a brief look.

- *Planning*

Planning and organizational skills are crucial components of the goal achievement process.

- *Clarity*

Having clarity around your goals will definitely put you on the right pathway. If your goals are vague then it will be difficult to get motivated. You need a clear vision. Goals can be made more specific through:

- Quantification - making it measurable. For example "$10,000 per month" instead of "make more money"
- Enumeration - defining tasks that need to be completed in order to achieve a goal. For example, "run every morning, to lose 5kg"

- *SMART +*

Make your goals fit into the SMART framework. That is they should be specific (S), measurable (M), achievable (A), realistic (R), timebound (T) and positive (+).

- *Motivation*

Motivation is what will encourage us to achieve a goal. Without the motivation goals are destined to fail. Which means you need to have goals that positively motivate you. It is imperative that goals are important and relevant on a personal level.

- *Time Management*

Goal setting relies heavily on being able to manage time well.

- *Flexibility*

Not all your plans will go as you expect. Sometimes you might have to divert from the planned method and go in another direction. A flexible attitude is necessary in this regard.

- *Persistence and focus*

Just as much as your plans might not go as you expect. Obstacles will also come your way and your motivation will go up and down. At those times you're going to need to stay persistent, focused and keep moving forward. Onwards and upwards.

- *Challenging*

Effective goal setting means you should set goals that are a little bit out of your reach yet they are still attainable. This will challenge you and require you to improve yourself. In turn that will give you the motivation to push your skills forward to their limits.

- *Self-regulation*

Goal setting can be challenging. Goals will and should test you to do what you didn't think was possible before. That will cause you to grow and become better. During that process you need to be able to regulate and manage your emotions so that you can deal with the challenges. This requires self-regulation.

- Vision

Your goals should paint a clear picture in your mind's eye. That vision must inspire you and be crystal clear.

- *Feedback*

Finally you need to have a good feedback system in place. That can be both internal and externa. Track and measure your results. This can be by yourself or you can also have a mentor to help you. Ultimately you need to know how you're progressing.

HOW TO SET GOALS

What should your goals be? Good question. Well some people might think life is all about money. Or life is about having a good time. In reality life has so many components to it. This is why I recommend you set goals in specific areas of your life. You want to live a full life right? Sometimes your health might not be good but you finanacial your situation is good. Or maybe have great relationships now but your career is not where you want it to be. Having a more balanced view of your life will help you to celebrate the wins in different areas. Let's take a closer look at the areas of your life.

Goal Setting Step 1

There are many sections here for you to set some goals for yourself in. If you want to add more go ahead. Live a full life. Brainstorm here and if you get stuck use some of the question prompts. Set a timer for five minutes on each section. No censorship, write as fast as you can.

Health

Health is the most important section. Without good health nothing else is really possible. Brainstorm this area and to help you consider the following questions.

- How do you want to look? How do you want to feel? Maybe you want to leap out of bed everyday. Or look and feel years younger than you really are. Whatever it is, write it down.

- How much do you want to weigh?

Maybe you want to lose a few kilos. Or maybe you want to bulk up and pack on the muscles.

- What do you want to accomplish?

That could be accomplishments such as lifting a certain amount of weight, competing in an event, running a distance or getting a martial arts grade.

- Are there any cosmetic procedures or surgeries you want?

Perhaps you want to enhance the way you look or take care of something that really bothers you. Don't be afraid to acknowledge this. If it's what you really want and not something just to fit in then write it down. It could be something simple as getting your teeth whitened or having a weekly facial.

- How often would you like to exercise?

Maybe you hate to exercise and want to do the least amount for the most gain. Or maybe you're a gym rat and you want to go all in.

- Are there any sports you want to try? Do you want to join a team or start up a new sport?

Relationships

Relationships give meaning to our life. Having someone to share life moments with makes life much more enjoyable. Think about what you're looking for in your relationships. Take five minutes to brainstorm and use the following questions to help you find clarity.

- What kind of relationship are you looking for?

Maybe you just want to date for a while. Or maybe you want to improve your existing relationship by committing to more dates, romance and better communication. Whatever you want.

- Do you want a better sex life?

Maybe this has been a concern of yours for a while and you want to improve it.

- Do you want a better romantic life?

Maybe your relationship has gone stale and it needs some new life breathed into it. Think about how you want to improve it.

- Do you want to get married? Have children?

Friends

Just like relationships, friends are equally important to living and sharing our best moments in life. Think about what you want here. Consider the following questions.

- What kind of social life do you want?

Maybe you want to attend more meetups, seminars and be out there everyday.

- What kind of friends do you want in your life?

Maybe you're tired of your old friends and you want to meet new people who inspire you. It could be meeting up with more like minded people on a regular basis or finding a mentor.

- What kind of social habits or skills would you like to develop?

Maybe it's simply saying hi to more people or working on your confidence.

Family

Family is another important part of our life. We need to give it the right amount of attention and not neglect. Family is important, it needs priority. Think about how you want your family life to be.

- Do you want to spend more time with your family? How much time and how often?

That could be moving closer to them or setting aside time each month or year to spend with them.

- Are there activities you want to do with your family? When? How often?

Maybe you love taking beach holidays with your parents or you just want to meet with your family for a weekly dinner.

- Do you want to have your own family?

Be specific about what you want. If you want ten kids then write it down. Dare to dream big.

Finance

Finance and money are the easiest things to quantify. They can help us directly measure our success and are a great indicator of it. Take the time to be specific about what you want. Dare to have big goals. Brainstorm and consider the following bullet points.

- How much money do you want to earn per month, per year? What would you like your salary to be?

Maybe you want to double your income and work less hours. Or maybe you want to get a better deal or even to quit your job. Would you like your paycheck to increase by a certain amount?

- How much money do you want to have saved?
Saving and growing your money is really important. Rainy days come and ultimately wealth is measured by net worth. Set what you want to go for.

- What investments would you like to make?
Having a bunch of money saved is good. But why not have it work for you? Study and research the most profitable and safest ways to invest. Make sure you understand any investment you make before you commit to it.

- Would you like to be completely debt-free?
If there are debts that bother you then write them out.

- Would you like to adopt positive beliefs about money?
Maybe you have some limiting beliefs around money that need fixing. Identify them.

- How many streams of income would you like to create? Would you like to start a business?
Maybe you're tired of the rate race and would like to build your own business on the side. Or you might have a great idea and want to go all in on it.

- When would you like to retire (at what age)?

- Would you like to be a multimillionaire?

Career

Most of our lives are spent working. But most of us are not working in jobs we enjoy. Think about your career and what you want to be, do and achieve. Take the time to brainstorm and consider the following questions.

- What do you want to achieve in your career?

Maybe right now you're not happy. You want to quit your job and change to a new career. Or it could be something like getting a promotion or making moves to start a business.

- Are there any professions out there that interest you?

We only live once so spend it doing what you enjoy. Don't chase the money, chase the passion and the money will follow.

- Do you want to go back to study or learn a useful work skill?

You're never too old or experienced to learn new things. That could mean completely reinventing yourself and going back to study a new skill. Allow yourself to make that possible.

Travel, passions and adventure

Travel, passions and adventures are the things that make us feel alive. They are what we love to do. Set your imagination free.

- Where do you want to travel to? How long do you want to spend there?

Travel is a great way to spend time. Think about where you most want to go. Maybe you want to spend a year backpacking or just a few weeks on a caribbean beach.

- What adventures do you want to go on?

Maybe you always wanted to jump out of a plane. Or climb a mountain. Dare to dream.

- How do you want to spend your free time?

Maybe you have always loved sailing and you want to spend your weekend out on the seas. Or maybe you love golf and want to be out on the course.

- What hobbies do you want to try?

Think about the hobbies you've always been curious about. Maybe you want to make music or learn to sing. Or maybe you want to learn how to cook.

Lifestyle

Lifestyle is about the quality of life you live. From the clothes you wear to the cars you drive, to the house you live in. Think big and set some goals.

What kind of place do you want to live in?
Maybe you want to live in a cottage in the countryside. Or maybe you want a fancy downtown apartment.

How would you like to travel?
Maybe you hate driving cars and you want a speed bike. Or maybe you want a new Porsche or you just want to be chauffeured around. Or even travel business class.

What kind of clothes do you want to wear?
Maybe being dressed in the latest designer fashion is important to you. Or maybe it's something as simple as looking good in nice fitting clothes.

Learning

Throughout life it's important to never stop learning

- Do you want to learn a new language?

Ever wanted to travel somewhere and speak with the locals. Considering learning a new language it can be an awesome skill to be able to communicate in a foreign country.

- Do you want to go back to study?

Maybe there is a hot new course you want to learn. Or you want to complete a masters.

- Do you want to learn anything else?

That could be anything from cooking to dressmaking to dancing. Whatever you want to learn, do it.

Spirituality/ Mental health

Mental health represents our state of mind. This is just as important as our physical body. Actions begin with thoughts and in order to be taking the right actions we need a healthy mind. Plus we need to be able to appreciate and enjoy life. Brainstorm and consider the following points. For some of us our faith is really important. For some of us we are curious about spirituality and faith. Or if it's not important to you then don't worry about it. But if you're curious or committed, take the time out to think about what you want. Brainstorm and consider the following.

- How do you want to feel?

Maybe you're tired of feeling depressed and you want to fix that. Or maybe you want to have a better attention span. Write down the things that bother you about mental health and set goals to fix them. Alternatively write out the ways you want to feel day to day.

- What activities do you want to do to improve your mental health?

Maybe you have always wanted to try meditation or brain training looks like a good idea to you. It could even be keeping a journal. Do a Google search to find some of the best ways to improve your mental health.

- Are you curious about any religions or spirituality?

Maybe you have always had a burning desire to seek out more knowledge on a spiritual journey. Whatever it is, take the path.

- Have you thought about doing a retreat or immersion?

Going on a retreat or immersion program can be one of the best ways to grow your faith and also improve your mental health. It could be something as simple as a yearly three day retreat.

Giving

Finally giving is really an important part of your goals. Some say the secret of living is giving. As you become more successful it's important to give something back and help others to achieve success. Brainstorm how you can give back?

- Are there any charities you want to support and how?

Maybe you want to set up a regular donation. Or even go and volunteer.

- What ways can you like to help others?

Again that could be donation, volunteering or even teaching valued skills to those in need.

Goal Setting Step 2

Ok so by now you should have a pretty big list of goals. Actually you should have a huge list of goals! Don't worry about the size of it too much though. Having a big list is better because ultimately we want to be living a full life. Now what I want you to do is to go through those lists of goals and next to them simply write, m, 3, 6, y, 5, 1. Those numbers and letters indicate the amount of years or months that you expect to achieve those goals. So for example;

- m = one month
- 3 = three months
- 6 = six months
- y = one year
- 5 = five years
- 10 = ten years or more.

Don't worry about being too exact just give a rough estimate. Take five to ten minutes to complete this activity. When you are done you should have a list with all the categories of time.

Organize

At this point I would suggest that you start to put your goals into some kind of Excel sheet. Personally my writing is ugly, so for me it works well to put my goals into Google sheets. However if you like to keep things more natural and you have some beautiful handwriting then by all means keep it inside of a notebook. Either way create a new page for each of the goal headings and then organize them by time.

Choose your top one year goals for each of the main categories. Look at all the one year goals in each category and select the ones that make you the most excited. Below those put like the short-term goals then at the very bottom the long-term goals. Those long-term goals will be a bit more vague but they will give you an overall picture of exactly what you're looking for long term.

Next, eliminate any goals that are not so important. Focus only on the goals that are most important to you. Put any others on the back burner in a tab somewhere. You can start to prioritise those with simple things such as A, B, or C.

Get SMART +

With your main one year goals in mind use the S.M.A.R.T. protocol which is a great system to help you move towards your goals and achieve them. It's essentially a framework that allows you to make sure your goals are optimised based on different properties.

Specific

Goals need to be specific otherwise it's just pie in the sky. That's not going to motivate you or drive you in the right direction. To help you make your goal specific try to answer the following questions.

- What is it that you want to accomplish?
- Why is your goal important?
- Who is involved?

- Where is the goal located?
- Which resources are required?

In addition going back to the earlier chapter consider quantification and enumeration.

- Quantification - making it measurable. For example "lose 5kg" instead of "look good"
- Enumeration - break the goal into specific steps. For example "invest in an index fund to grow my net worth"

Measurable

To keep you motivated, on track and making progress you need to have measurable goals. When you're able to assess and measure your progress it will help you to stay focused, meet your deadlines and get excited about moving closer to achieving your goal. In order to turn your goal into something measurable, consider the following questions

- How much?
- How many?
- How will I know when my goal is accomplished?

Example
Let's say your goal is to get a promotion at your company. That can be measured by taking on the necessary training and then finally getting that promotion.

Achievable

True goals need to be challenging but they should not be completely unrealistic. The perfect goals should stretch your abilities yet still be possible. For example if you're a middle-aged guy then breaking the 100m world record is rather unrealistic. But you could for example work towards breaking your own records or even local ones. To help you set an achievable goal consider the following questions.

- How realistic is this goal based on my current situation?
- Realistically, could I accomplish this goal?
- What sacrifices would I have to make?
- Am I willing to make those sacrifices?

Tip
You can achieve much more than you think so don't be afraid to go for it. When I first started making money online I was realistic and set the goal to make just $1 online. When I achieved that it motivated me to shoot a bit higher. I kept doubling and going higher until I reached something that at the beginning was way beyond my wildest dreams. Start small and keep growing.

Relevant

Make sure that your goals matter to you and align with your vision for your life. On the journey towards your goals you will likely need support from people and your environment. Make sure they are aligned with your goals and also who you are as a person. If they don't then you need to consider making changes to either your goals, the people around you or your environment. Are you willing to do that? To make sure that your goals are relevant consider the following questions.

- Does this motivate me?
- What will it require??
- What kind of people could help me?
- What kind of environment do I need to be in?

- Am I willing to do what it takes?
- Is now the right time?

Example

Maybe you have the dream to travel the world or to visit ten countries in the next six months. However if the whole world is on lockdown for whoever knows how long then that is going to be impossible. In that case you might want to either delay that goal or to change it to something more relevant. For example, planning and saving or travelling within your home country.

Time-bound

In the end everyone needs to have a target date for their goals. A deadline for you to focus on and work towards. This will light a fire underneath you and motivate you to prioritise what gets results. Work either expands or contracts according to how much time is set for it. Be realistic about this but also make it a challenge for yourself. To turn your goal into something time based and answer the following questions.

- When is a realistic but challenging time to achieve this goal?
- What can I do right now?
- What is possible 1 months from now?
- What is possible 6 months from now?

Example

Maybe you're looking to compete in a small local bodybuilding competition. You want to get on the stage and look your best. Today that could involve going to the gym and eating clean. In one month that could mean bulking your physique up through a high protein intake and heavy lifting. In six months it could be cutting down, losing fat and getting a toned body. During the process you could be taking pictures and measuring your results every month, week and so on.

+ Finally make your goals positive and present

The human mind is particularly sensitive to negativity and positivity. It's been proven that it's best to put your goals into the positive, present tense. Instead of having goal statements such as "I don't want to be fat" you need to be more positive and state something such as "I look and feel my best" so take a look at your goals and turn anything that looks negative into something positive in the present. Having them in the present tense also makes them more believable and less vague. When you look at your goals they should inspire you and motivate you to go for them.

EXAMPLES OF GOAL SETTING

Ok so if you struggled with the last chapter then I want you to take a look at this chapter. Here I'm going to give you some examples of goal setting. But if you didn't struggle with the last chapter and you're already well on your way then you can ignore this chapter and skip to the next one. Anyway I suggest you take a look either way.

Health

Susan is not really happy with the way she looks and feels. After a shower she looks in the mirror and isn't happy with what she sees. A little bit too much fat around the sides and a little too many wrinkles. In her mind she wants to "look younger and fitter". That's great but it's not really specific, measurable or time based. Although it is achievable and relevant so at least two boxes are ticked. Now on the time side of things this could be a great one year goal. She could already start making it specific by taking a look at her current age and height. Then by just doing some Google searches for people or celebrities of similar ages and heights that she wants to look like. She can find out what their weight and routines are. Then she has a rough idea of the weight she wants to be and what actions are required. Ok so that's one and then she can start to enumerate on that and figure out the right steps. Plus she now has something to measure and a strong vision to guide her forwards.

Relationships

For the last two years of his relationship Brian has not been happy. He always argues with his wife Mary. Ever since the kids left home it's like they are always clashing and getting in each other's ways. Brian and Mary still love each other but it's not realized enough. Frustrated, Brian decides to take action and make it a priority to bring the love back to their relationship. Recognizing this is the first step and the motivation is there. Brian talks with Mary about the times they cherished before the kids were born. The walks together, visiting people and going out for dinners. They agree to now make it a priority to have more unique and special moments together. Brian successfully set a goal. He made it specific and measurable because he can count how many special moments he shares with his wife. Plus it's completely relevant and achievable. Together they can work on expanding those moments to better and more grand activities. This will bring the love back to the relationship.

Finance

William had drifted from job to job for the past six years. Sometimes he would make a decent amount of money but then there would be months of low wages and he would just end up spending the savings. He hated relying on being an employee. Fed up he looked for a new way. He did his research and was inspired by people making money online and being their own boss. He decided that he wanted to build his own source of income and to be completely location independent. His vision was to be financially and location independent within one year. The next step for him was to make it more specific. He set about making a realistic income and this could be measured to make sure he was on target. That figure was always achievable for him and when he hit that target he would increase it. This helped to keep him motivated. Plus it was time bound. In addition he made sure to always keep his goal set in the positive tense so that his mind was inspired.

Learning

Claire was finishing up her bachelor of arts at Cardiff University. For the summer she planned to volunteer at a local school in Thailand. Claire had never been to Thailand before and she decided it would be a good idea to learn the language. With an idea in mind, Claire set herself the goal to become fluent in conversational Thai language within three months. The goal fit well within the SMART protocol. It was specific and could be measured by how well she conversed. Achievable and realistic also yes because it wasn't so unrealistic that there was not enough time to learn. Finally it was time bound by three months. Next the plan and feedback system could easily fit into place as she could brainstorm the actions and feedback points for the goal. For example she could use apps, books and then measure her progress by how well she conversed with locals or graded on tests.

BE RUTHLESS

One of the biggest obstacles to achieving your goals is the other goals that you have. Each goal is competing for time and attention from each other. When you commit to one goal you're taking the focus and energy from another. To achieve your most important goals requires a ruthless attitude. Take advice from Warren Buffett who has been consistently ranked as one of the most wealthy people in the world. Clearly he knows how to manage and spend his time each day. To help his employees decide upon their main priorities he uses a three step productivity strategy.

The first step is to write down your goals. Since we've already done that we can skip ahead to step two - choose your top five goals. Go through the lists of the different goals you set and choose the five most important to you.

Step three, anything that you did not choose is not urgent. These goals should be avoided at all costs otherwise they will just take your time and focus away from your main goals. Wasting time on secondary goals is the main reason you have half-finished projects instead of completed ones. Eliminate ruthlessly and force yourself to focus on what matters.

The Four Burners Theory

Imagine a cooking stove with four burners on it. Each burner represents a quadrant of your life. This is a concept known as The Four Burners Theory. The Four Burners Theory states that for you to be successful you have to cut off one of your burners. But to be really successful you have to cut off two of your burners.

- Burner one represents your family
- Burner two represent your friends
- Burner three represents your health
- Burner four represents your work

Now I know what you're thinking. There must be some way that I can succeed and keep all of those four burners running, right? Maybe you could combine two. For example you could start a business with your wife and kids and then you can combine family and work. Or you could switch jobs to be a fitness instructor and then you're making money and taking care of yourself at the same time right? Sure that's all good but you're still not facing the issue at hand. Which is that life is full of trade offs. If you really want to excel in one area then you need to make sacrifices in another area. For example if you want to be a family man then you're going to need to step back from your career ambitions a little bit. Or if you want to do it the other way round then you are going to be spending less time at home and sacrifice moments with your family. You can divide time equally amongst those burners but you have to accept that you won't reach your full potential in all of those areas.

Which means you need to make choices. Do you want to live a life that is out of balance but very successful in one area? Or would you rather live a balanced life but never truly live up to your full potential in any of those areas? Now don't worry because there are some ways you can still excel and be balanced. One way is that you can outsource some of those burners. There are so many small things in our lives that we can outsource. We can get delivery food so that we don't have to cook. We can pay someone to take care of our laundry. We can hire a nanny to take care of our kids. We can pay a virtual assistant to take care of tasks that we don't want to do in our business. Things like this free us to spend time on more meaningful activities. Essentially it keeps the burning running without you wasting unnecessary time on it.

Another option you have concerns the time available in your life. When thinking of The Four Burners Theory it can be frustrating to think, "if only I had more time". Well the way around that is to maximise the time you have. Each of us have our own set of constraints and limitations on our time. Maybe that's working from nine to five every day. Or having family, exercise and various other commitments every day. What you need to ask yourself is, am I being as effective as possible here? For example if you only have one hour to work out each day ask yourself what is the most effective way to reach my goal during this time? Or if I have my evenings to spend with my family what is the best way to spend quality time with them?

Be ruthless with your self examination. Lines of questioning like this focus us to make the most of the time available. Instead of worrying about negativity and not having enough time your focus will be on the quality of time spent. After all isn't it better to spend one hour of quality romantic time with your partner then an evening of watching meaningless stuff on Netflix? Wouldn't it be better to smash a workout in thirty minutes as opposed to scrolling through your phone intermittently during an average one hour workout?

Finally another way to manage the four burners theory is by breaking time into the seasons of life. Break the balances between the burners to different periods of time where you focus more on one particular area during a period of time. That can change throughout your life. For example in your twenties and thirties you're probably going to be single and so it's going to be easier to hit the gym and chase your career ambitions. That's when those health and work burners will be full whilst family and friends are turned down. Then years later you might want to turn down those burners and turn up the family burners. Later on you might turn them up again as your children grow up and you have more time to spend on work pursuits. It could even mean periods of immersion. Such as taking out three months to write your new book. Or a year off to spend time with your family and newborn child. You can have those other burners in maintenance mode and always come back to them later on.

TURN YOUR DREAMS INTO REALITY

Goals can seem daunting but if you have an actionable plan in place it can increase the chances of making them much more likely to achieve. Plans are the blueprint to get you from where you are now to where you want to be in the future. A plan of action consists of all the actions, activities, habits and so on that are essential to successfully achieving your goal. This turns your goal into quantifiable actions that can be mapped out on a timeline. Included inside will be ordered necessary steps required to achieve your goals. You can break that huge overwhelming goal into single or multiple goals.

It's been proven that you're much more likely to stick to your goals when you have a specific plan for them. Think about the when, where and how. There are specific benefits to planning. Number one it improves your productivity. A plan is going to stop you wasting your time and energy on unnecessary tasks. Every minute you spend will be on executing something important. This will also give you more focus and help you to feel more in control of your life. In turn this affects your confidence because you're moving forward and it proves that your plans are working. Finally it gives you greater self-awareness because it helps you to understand yourself and your life priorities.

With your goals in mind you need to figure out the daily, weekly and monthly activities that you need to complete in order to make them happen. Select your goals and break them down into clearly defined steps. If you followed the steps before and you set SMART goals then it's going to be easy for you to break your goals down into actionable steps.

Brainstorm and list every action step that needs to happen for you to achieve your goal. Figure out the people resources and materials that you need to complete your goal. Identify the daily or weekly habits that will move you closer towards your goal. For example if you want to get ripped then that's going to the gym and eating clean everyday. Or if you want to save more money than that's measuring your daily and weekly spending. Select what actions need to happen from the first to the last. Make sure that all of the actions are relevant and attainable in regard to your goal. If the action seems too big or overwhelming then it can be broken down into smaller actions.

- Work backwards, step by step from achieving your goal
- Brainstorm and list every action that needs to happen
- Figure out the people, resources and materials that you need
- Identify the daily, weekly or monthly habits that will move you closer
- Set time frames and use a calendar to help you

Along with having a deadline for your goal you also need a time frame for each action within your goal. This will ensure you are consistently progressing towards your goal. For each action step, assess what's required and then consider the amount of time that you need to complete the action. Be realistic and think about all of the obstacles and activities involved when you're selling a timeframe. Then set dates for each action and put those into your calendar to remind you.

Keep your plans together in some kind of planner. You should be looking at your goals everyday and reviewing them. Personally I recommend Google sheets and a calendar. This allows me to check in on my goals everyday either on my mobile or laptop from wherever I am in the world. I can update the goals as I progress. I recommend you keep a tab for each of your goals. So on one tab for example you could have health goals, then another finance and so on. On each of those tabs you can break down those goals into the actions you need to take each day, week, each month and so on. Monitor your progress on an available column.

Habits

Habits are automatic actions which means that not much thought goes into them. This makes it easy for you to quickly accomplish goals with ease. For example if you develop the habit of going to the gym everyday then that's a huge win for you. Or if your goal is to be more confident and you make it a habit of talking to strangers then that is an excellent habit.

Taking things further we can stack our habits. Stacking habits means that when we take one particular action it causes us to take another particular action. For example when you make your morning coffee it's a trigger for you to meditate. This then triggers you to do some stretching. Through habit stacking you can really start to implement a fully blown plan moving towards your goals with little effort!

Align Your Environment With Your Goals

To give yourself a good advantage, make your environment support your goals. Our decisions are often based on the environment that we find ourselves in. The decisions we make both personally and professionally are influenced by the options that are around us. For example if you use your mobile phone as an alarm clock then you'll be more likely to check your notifications when you wake up. If you hang out with people that like to get wasted every weekend then you're more likely to drink. If you have a huge 50inch TV inside your bedroom then you're more likely to spend most of your time watching it. Get the point?

Now those are all environments that can have negative implications on your life. So why not become more conscious of your environment and how it affects you? For example if health is important to you then make sure you live close to a gym or have some exercise equipment nearby. Make sure that you have healthy food options in your place. If you are tired of getting wasted every Friday night then set up something more productive to do such as a night class or going on a date with someone you like.

Try to boil things down to the simplest of essence and cut out the noise. If you have tons of distractions around you all the time it's going to make it very difficult to focus on what's important. Eliminate those decisions and distractions. Sometimes you might have to remove certain things completely. Maybe that's blocking certain websites on your browser. Or it's about limiting the kind of food that you're going to eat. Be ruthless.

Keep an organised and tidy environment. There have been numerous studies proving that untidy environments distract us from what we're doing. For this reason you should maintain a clean and tidy workspace. Make sure everything is in order and this will help you to stay focused. Every minute of your day matters so establish an optimised environment. Clear up your desk, put things away and organise your notes. In the same regard you need to eliminate mental distractions. Those can be the smallest thing such as background noise or having multiple tabs open on your computer. Or if you have people that are constantly interrupting, telephone calls, texts and so on then remove those distractions. Establish some boundaries and rules during your working hours. Maybe that means deleting social media and going somewhere that will allow you to be more productive.

MOTIVATION & TIME

Now excuse the hype and I don't want to be too unrealistic about it but I want to stay something. Most goals are possible to achieve if they are somewhat realistic. The reason why people are unsuccessful with goal setting is that they have a vague romantic idea of a goal. Maybe they read a motivational quote and got super motivated but never followed through. Again we come back to the SMART theory which is to say that you need to stick with the real, actionable specific goals.

Motivation is one of the biggest influences on successfully achieving a goal. Goals get people started and motivation gives them the energy to get things done. The combination results in success. The psychologist Edwin Locke in the 1960s proposed the theory of motivation in goal setting. His theory states that goal setting and task performance are linked to each other. Essentially this states that by having challenging goals your motivation will be higher.

You are your own best motivator and your motivation must come from within yourself. Regardless of encouragement, the only one who can achieve your goals is you. But how do you stay motivated? Here's how:

- *Set boundaries*

Be realistic here. True, you can work your face off but at some point you're going to get burned out. You need to be able to push yourself hard but you don't want to get so burned out that you never want to go again. For example if you're trying to lose weight maybe you run two days in a row and then the next day you have off or maybe you have a cheat day on a Sunday. Or maybe you're working so much on a project and then take time off to spend with your lover. Set yourself some simple boundaries and that will keep you motivated because you know that there will be a break coming up instead of endless work.

- *Break it down*

There's a famous saying "how do you eat an elephant? One bite at a time." Think about your goals in the same way. Big goals need to be taken one step at a time. Say for example if your goal is to be a business owner then you need to set some small actions first such as research, cutting down your hours, investing and so on. Think what your goal is and break it down into more manageable pieces. You should have done this in the chapter before but I just want to push that point home again because it will keep you motivated with small wins.

- *Minimize distractions*

Distractions will keep you from your goals. Nothing will get done that is meaningful. If you find yourself constantly distracted then maybe you're not very motivated by your goals and you need to revisit them. Otherwise you can minimize your distractions through elimination. The truth is focus is not really about optimization it's more about subtraction. So for example if you have things distracting you such as the TV or social media then you can block them or remove them from your environment. Again as we discussed, optimize your environment to have less distractions and you'll be able to get more done.

- *Education*

A thirst for knowledge is an excellent quality to have. Many times people get fed up and give up because they feel like they're not intelligent enough to achieve their goal. That is simply just a matter of education. If you feel you're not progressing fast enough just ask yourself do I have the appropriate knowledge? Incidentally you don't want to get lost in knowledge. Taking action is the most important step. But if there are areas that you feel that you don't have the adequate knowledge in then get educated. Study the relevant books, enroll yourself in a course or even hire a mentor and acquire all the relevant knowledge.

- *Waste no time*

Start right now on your goals. The best thing you can do for any goal that you set it to take a definitive action right away. If you want to get fit and healthy, go do some push ups right now. If you want to meet the partner of your dreams, sign up for an online dating site or go out and start meeting people. If you want to make money online then start researching how to do that. Do it now! Light the fire underneath you and take action right away. Waste no time and you will become motivated by your actions.

- *Embrace failure*

Failure is a part of success. Ask any successful person and they'll probably tell you that their failures by far outweigh their successes. The difference between them and the people who don't achieve their goals is that the latter give up. The successful realize that failure is part of the equation and it doesn't affect their motivation. It just makes them more motivated to try again and succeed at all costs. Think about it like the stock market. The only time you lose is when you sell (give up).

Time Management

Time management skills are crucial in goal setting. A person who manages their time wisely has a much better chance of achieving their goals than one who doesn't. If you don't have good time management skills then you might make some small progress towards your goals but you will never achieve your best results. Your best results rely on effective time management. Whether you're young or old time is the greatest equaliser for all of us. Yet so many people fail to achieve their goals because they didn't manage their time well. They procrastinated, they didn't prioritise and they didn't put together a proper time management plan. Essentially they wasted time, but life is too short for you to waste time.

Time management will give you more control over how you spend every moment of your life allowing you to spend more time doing what you love and what gets results. Doesn't that sound good? Of course it does, because ultimately that's how you can achieve your goals. There really are no negatives, only benefits. Benefits such as less procrastination. Having a schedule will provide you with a framework to go for what's really important to you and to cut out those things that are taking you away from your purpose. Stick to a good plan and your calendar. Then you can start to become really effective, implement a routine and build successful habits. When there's less procrastination in your life you're more likely to meet deadlines, get things done and achieve your goals.

Additionally this will cause you to work smarter. Through practice you'll be able to implement proper time management and set realistic deadlines which will give you the motivation to push forward when you achieve them. In turn you become more accountable for yourself and your results because you'll be analysing your own time spent. Through this time management and measurement you'll be able to tune into what gives you the best results and in turn have even better time management.

A side benefit of good time management skills is that you will be less stressed because you will have more free time to chill out and relax. Going at full speed all the time is going to eventually burn you out. You need time to unwind and let your brain cool down. Make sure you are living a well balanced life. Take breaks and avoid burnout. Good time management skills and techniques will allow you more time to focus on taking care of your mental health which is at the core of being a successful goal achiever. This lifts a burden of stress and anxiety from your shoulders. We need to be driven but also calm and collected to achieve our goals. To help you practice better time management here are some helpful tips.

- *Know your goals*

First and foremost make sure your goals are crystal clear. The earlier chapters should have helped you to ensure your goals meet those requirements. Now if you're still unsure then go back and do the exercise again. Otherwise you'll just be shooting for some vague concepts and that will cause a lot of procrastination. Make sure they meet the SMART criteria: Specific, Realistic, Achievable, Realistic, Time-Bound.

- *Track your time*

In order to be effective you need to understand where your time is being spent. Now you don't need to do this all the time. But I would suggest that for one week you track every hour of the day. You can set an alarm on your phone to go off every hour to remind you to write down what you are doing at that moment. Keep a log of it all. At the end of the week you can analyze where your time was spent, what you accomplished and if your time was well spent. Are you happy with the results? Do you need to improve? Are there activities that need to be removed? I suggest you do this every few months or so to make sure that you keep becoming more effective in the way you spend your time.

Prioritise

Every day you need to be working on your goals. By now you should have your goals mapped out in a planner. Every day you're going to need to set some tasks and actions to take towards achieving your goals. What I recommend you do is that at the end of every day or in the morning go through those goals and write down the top six most important things that you need to get done. Limit yourself to just six things. That will really trigger you to be hyper focused on what's a priority and what's really important to you.

Next pull up those six tasks and concentrate only on the first task. Do not stop working until that task is complete. Upon completion you can move on to the next task. Approach the whole list in the same fashion, never moving on to another task before you have completed the one task. At the end of the day you should have completed all of the six actions. If you haven't don't worry, put them onto the next day's plan and keep grinding towards success.

Earlier I mentioned choosing your six most important tasks to do for the next day. Well this is all about making priorities. Going further on that, the first action should be one of the hardest things to do and also the most beneficial. At the start of your day you will be at your freshest with full willpower.

Place your activities into four different sections based on urgency and importance. Just write out a box with four sections for each of those parts and then you can enter your actions. Alternatively you can use the simple prioritising method on a list. Write a number or letter next to each item and then organize by ascending priority. Use the time management quadrant below to help you prioritize.

Urgent and important (do)	Not urgent but important (plan)
Urgent but not important (delegate)	Not urgent and not important (eliminate)

- *Set time limits*

Some activities can go on forever if you let them. Things like checking emails or running advertising campaigns can just consume so much time. Instead it's better to limit the time spent. Block out time to do those activities and then set a timer. Work on those activities until that timer goes off. Not only will this give you hyperfocus but it will also create an excellent management of your time.

- *Say no*

Protecting your time is crucial. Sometimes it's ok for you to say no. For example if your boss asks you to do something that's not particularly urgent you might want to tell him that this is going to take you away from doing more meaningful activities. Instead delegate it. Or maybe your friends ask you out to drink beer but you want to work on your business. If there are projects not working out with people don't be afraid to walk away. By saying no to certain things it will free you up to focus your efforts on the things that matter.

Flexibility

As we discussed earlier when you set a goal you also create a plan to get there. But that plan shouldn't be so rigid that it doesn't have flexibility for unexpected opportunities and obstacles along the way. There's a famous quote that says the map is not the territory. This is a metaphor that can be applied to goals and planning The plan is the map but that doesn't mean it accurately reflects what's going to happen in real life. Things will happen that are unexpected. To deal with those we need to be flexible and sometimes take a different pathway. Or sometimes adjust your goal to maybe get something much better. Always be open to those opportunities and flexible on your path.

Stay fresh

Finally I want to tell you something that's pretty important. Stay fresh without judgment and without ego. It can be easy to get jaded and want to give up when things don't go the way you want. But if you can keep a clean slate in your mind that can really help to easily bring new opportunities to you.

Multi billionaire Richard Branson says "think like a child to get a head". Richard Branson is quite a unique person. After dropping out of school at the age of sixteen he went on to set up his own business Empire. He has said that a fresh mind is the cause of much of his success. Just like a child he can see opportunities where adults often see obstacles. This is exactly the mindset that he had when he quit his studies and first set up his first company as a teenager. He let go of ego or judgement and embraced the inner child. He leapt into the unknown. Throughout his career he has maintained that childlike attitude from launching Virgin Records to Virgin

Atlantic airline and more. He has even said that there were many times he didn't know what he was doing but just like a child he pushed through and achieved what seemed impossible.

"If your ego and your accomplishments stop you from listening, then they've taught you nothing." Jimmy Iovine.

<u>NEVER GIVE UP</u>

Whatever your goals are you need to persist at them and stay focused. Nothing can take the place of persistence. You might be talented but without persistence you won't get anywhere. Most goals don't come true because people give up. They meet a challenge or setback and they don't persist. There are reasons for that. First and foremost you need to have a reason behind your persistence. No one wants to keep going if they don't care about the result. We need to make sure our goals have meaning and matter to us. Never set goals just to please others or to look good. Really put thought into the why of your goals. Question them and write down why they matter to you. If the why behind them is not strong enough reason then revisit your goals.

Self belief is another reason that people do not achieve their goals. In order to achieve anything we need self belief. Now part of the SMART acronym that we looked at earlier states that goals should be achievable and realistic. But that doesn't mean you should set small goals. They should be something big enough to inspire you and also believable for you to achieve. If it's something too lofty then you're going to get discouraged and you won't persist. To really win, break down a big goal into lots of small goals. Those can be like your milestones on the journey towards the big goal. Staying with the SMART acronym for a moment remember to measure your goals. When we lose sight of how far we've come it can be easy to get discouraged. Through measuring our goal accomplishments it's going to inspire us to motivate us to move forward. Not only will you cultivate persistence you will also cultivate momentum. Get those wins under your belt.

To really ensure your maximum persistence surround yourself with a team of people that will inspire you to move forward. Great achievements have never been achieved alone. there's no such thing as a self-made man or woman. Just think of people like Arnold Schwarzenegger. He was helped by Joe Wilder at the start of his bodybuilding career. Joe introduced him to America, the gyms, trainers, methods and helped to make him a household name. Or think of Taylor Swift who was inspired by Shania Twain's songs. There are two types of relationships that can help you to persist through adversity and achieve your goals.

- *Mentors*

Mentors are a guide to your goals. They are people who have usually gone through the process before and achieved something similar to what you're trying to achieve. They'll be able to look at your strengths and weaknesses from a bird's eye view and pinpoint exactly what you need to do. You might not actually need to have met them in person. They could come from reading biographies, YouTube videos, listening to music and so on.

- *Peers*

Peers are the people at a similar level that are facing similar situations and challenges. They are your friends and colleagues. They will give you confidence and support towards solutions and innovations. With a team of mentors and peers in place it will help you to progress forward even during the most challenging of times.

Vision boards

Vision boards are one of the most valuable tools available to you. They form a visual representation of where you're going.

Through feeding your subconscious mind with these images it brings you closer to achieving your destiny. The human mind is easily influenced by visual stimulus and therefore representing your goals using images stimulates your emotions much more than words. After all, words can only say so much. A picture can say much more.

A vision board is a collection of images that represent your goals. The collection can be a cork board with pins of pictures printed out and pinned onto it. Or it could even be something made on your computer and then saved as an image. Regardless of where you store it by placing your goals in visual form it allows you to study them frequently and install them deep into your awareness. This focuses your mind on your goals and attracts you to the right situations and opportunities.

The vision board is the perfect tool for keeping your goals at the top of your mind. Ideally you want to put that vision board somewhere that you can see everyday and that will encourage you to frequently visualise your goals. This is a really important step to take because your subconscious mind is fed by these visions which programme your brain to be aware of opportunities. It will magnetise and attract the right people, opportunities and resources towards achieving your goal. Plus you will become naturally more motivated to reach your goals. Surprisingly you'll find yourself in more situations that bring you closer to your goals. This is all due to programming your subconscious through the visualization.

How to create a vision board

First of all pull up your goals. Start finding pictures that represent those goals, the feelings around them and the experiences. Look through magazines, newspapers and Google to find the right images. Choose images that inspire you and make you feel good. Be selective and tidy about what you put on the board. Don't put too much on there. It should be clear to you. Too many images will dilute your focus. For example if you've always dreamt of having a house by the beach then try to find an image of that that really resonates with you. Or if you've always wanted an amazing body, find a picture of an amazing body and just cut the head off it and put it on your health board. whatever represents that goal to you and whatever speaks and resonates put it in there. Additionally I like to put some affirmations, inspirational words, quotes and so on on the boards. Those can represent how you want to feel. It could be emotions you want to feel on a daily basis such as, happy, loved, healthy, free and so on.

If you're creating a hard copy vision board then print or cut them out. If you are just creating an online canvas then canva is a great tool which is free to use. They have some cool templates to fit your pictures into multiple grids on one page. Personally I have a page for each of my goals with various images of relevance. For example one for the career, one for health and so on. Work on your vision board and regularly update it. Keep those goals you achieved in there also because that proves you can do it.

Everyday take a few moments to contemplate your vision board. Make sure you're getting the full benefit of it so place it somewhere that you'll see every day. I suggest that you take a few minutes to look at it at least twice a day. When you wake up it is a good time and when you go to bed is also a good time. This will make sure that your goals are at the top of your mind when you start the day and that they are programmed into your subconscious while sleeping. If it's a hard copy try leaving it in your bedroom. if it's a data version then you can have it as your desktop background or on your spreadsheet with all your goals inside. Wherever it is just make sure that you see it everyday.

Go ahead and give the vision board a try, you've got nothing to lose. At the very least it will give you an idea of what you're looking for more clearly. That will stop your goals from being so vague. What we focus on expanding our lives. Visualisation is one of the most effective ways to expand on the things that we want to focus on. Get clear on your goals and motivate yourself to bring them into reality.

Write your goals everyday

Writing out your goals every morning is a great way to further install them into your subconscious. There is something about the act of writing goals out by hand that connects the mind and your focus. Numerous studies have proven this. For a number of years I have been doing this. In fact the first thing I do every morning is to write out my top goals. At that time of the day your subconscious mind is primed for manifesting goals.

If you're still not sure of what your goals are you can use this exercise to just write out whatever you want everyday for the next thirty days. At the end of thirty days you will notice that there are some consistently written goals. Those are your main goals.

Affirmations

In the same regard affirmations are another great way to install your goals into your goal seeking subconscious. If you followed the goal setting process in this book so far then your goals should be written in the present tense and in a positive tone. In addition, create more affirmations of the kind of person who would achieve those goals. For example,

Goal = Lose 5 kg. Affirmations = I am 80kg, I am slim and fit, I am healthy
Goal = Double my salary. Affirmations = I am earning 10k usd per month, I am wealthy, I am smart
Goal = Find my perfect partner. Affirmations = I am in a happy relationship, I am the prefer partner, I am confident
Goal = Travel to Egypt. Affirmations = I am travelling to Egypt, I am adveteturus.

You can recite those goals out loud everyday. I suggest doing it every morning and night before bed. You can really go all in it by doing them every hour. Sometimes I do this for ten days. I will have an alarm go off every hour and that will be my cue to recite affirmations or write out my goals. After ten days my mind is much more positively in tune. I invite you to take this challenge.

TEAMS & ACADEMIA & MORE

Goal setting is an important part of any successful organisation. The goals of each employee should align with the goals of the company. Team leaders and managers must take responsibility for communicating the goals of the organization to their team. They also need to encourage employees to set and link their individual goals to align with the vision of the company as a whole.

Setting the right goals for your team is probably the most important part of the goal setting process. Achieving the desired outcome for the company depends on it. Many employees struggle to understand their team's strategies. As a result of this disconnect many don't care. According to research by Robert Kaplan and David Norton less than ten percent of employees fully understand what is expected of them and what their company strategy is. Teams need to drive clear communication of values, goals and vision are integral to a successful culture.

Setting goals for your team is an undeniably important activity to create a united effort towards success. When your team has specific and challenging goals it will inspire higher levels of performance. Everyone will be closer aligned and working towards the same vision. Failure to effectively set goals for your team will result in poor results and productivity of your employees. Your team needs to know why they are given a task where it fits into a larger vision.

Clearly there are some significant benefits to goal setting. Not only will it boost your employee engagement it will also save you time and improve efficiency. Goal setting in your team will make sure the team is all on the same path. They all know what's expected of them and it creates a harmonious culture. Everyone has an equal responsibility and duty. People will have a wide understanding behind the purpose of what they are doing. As such they will take care in what they are doing because they appreciate the value of their work. This will keep your team motivated and encourage them to work harder. Plus the high achievers will be more likely to help out their peers with any issues that may arise.

To further strengthen relationships team leaders should regularly arrange team building activities. Those will break tensions and make the team more comfortable with each other. It will also help the team to understand each other's strengths and weaknesses. At all times open communication must be encouraged and misunderstandings dealt with promptly. The end result for the team is to become better and stronger.

Successfully setting goals in a team depends on having alignment between the objectives of the team and at an individual level. In a nutshell everyone needs to be working towards the same vision. Make sure your team understands the team's goals and encourage them to set goals for themselves and the group. Ask them to consider what they want to achieve and how will it benefit the team? Ensure that they are motivated. Goals shouldn't just be about the outcome it should involve a fulfilling process for all involved. The key is to cover three things, the end result, the measurement and the why.

There are a number of methods you can use when setting goals in teams. The SMART methodology explained earlier is just as effective for setting goals individually as it is for teams.

OKR is another method you can use. More on that later. To help you set goals for your team consider using a customised system that has attributes to suit your company.

OKR

OKR (Objectives and Key Results) is a useful and easy to use goal system used by Google and more. The concept originated in Silicon Valley with Google adopting it in 1999. Since then Google has grown from forty employees to over sixty thousand. In addition to Google using OKR, other companies including Walmart, Spotify, Target, Twitter, LinkedIn and more use it.

Through setting measurable goals it can be used to create alignment and engagement. Application of OKR ensures that goals are frequently set, tracked and evaluated. This is perfect in corporate and working environments because it really engages the whole team. Making sure that everyone is headed in the same direction with clarity is a strong advantage of the method.

The formula for OKR requires that a goal describes both what you will achieve and how you will measure it. The goal is the target and how you measure it makes it. Without these components it is just a dream. The formula for OKR goes as follows.

I will _____ as measured by _____.

Fill in the blanks and you have your goal/target and measurement. You can have multiple measures if you need to. For example your goal could be to increase commissions in your company by a certain amount and that could be measured by customer acquisition. Or another example could be a sales target from your advertising campaigns. That could be measured by conversions of the advertising. You could even start to use OKR in your personal life. For example, say you want to have a relationship but your single. That's your goal and measuring it could be from dates you went on. Or one more example could be health. Say you want to gain 5kg of muscle. Well you could measure that goal by weight gain or gym attendance.

As we can see the acronym OKR has two key components. Objectives which are your goals and key results which are your measurements. The objectives should be clear, quality and engaging so that they motivate you and your team. The key results should also be clear, quantitative and measurable. Essentially it should be a number. They can be multiple but not too many otherwise people will get lost in the system.

The uniqueness of OKR is that it can be adapted and tweaked. Instead of the standard static plans that many companies use OKR takes a more flexible approach to goal setting. Through using shorter goal cycles it makes companies much more able to adapt and respond to changes. Not only that but OKR is simple and straightforward to implement. Goals don't need to be a laborious process which is usually the case when more people are involved. OKR reduces the time spent setting goals and as a result their resources are driven towards achievement instead of planning.

Introducing OKR to your team is more of a journey than an event. Changes in culture of a company does not happen overnight. Company dynamics should be modified over a few months as you customize the new system into place. An important part of OKR is to ensure everyone understands what's expected of them at work. The information should be clear to all involved so that everyone moves towards the same goals and is on the same page. When correctly set up, OKRs are a simple process and won't take up much time to implement. In most cases it will only take a few hours each quarter to check and review your OKRs.

OKR Tips

- Typically set during the quarterly planning process.
- Lightweight and not time consuming
- Productivity, focus, and great for company culture.
- Flexible

Objectives:

- Consist of 3-5 high level Objectives.
- Should be simple, short and easy to memorize
- Make sure they are fun and motivate your team.

Key Results:

- Consist of 3-5 measurable Key Results
- Measured by a number or a score, 0-100% or 0 to 1.0.
- Quantifiable, achievable and not impossible.

THE FEEDBACK LOOP

In 1953 it was starting to look impossible that the world's highest mountain, Mount Everest could be climbed. Since 1921 ten attempts to climb the mountain had all failed. Analysis of those failures revealed that the climbers were not taking the right pathway up the mountain. In 1950 a new southern pathway to summit the mountain through Nepal was discovered. A new way had been found through feedback.

The first to attempt through the new pathway was by a Swiss team in 1952. They climbed all the way up to 228,210 feet before going back down. This was the highest anyone had been so far. Their failure to summit the mountain was down to persistence and fitness. Enter a beekeeper Edmund Hillary (later Sir Edmund). At thirty three years old Edmund was a strong candidate. In the past two years he had been on four Himalayan expeditions and was at the prime of his physical fitness. Aware of the shortcomings of the previous exhibitions he came fit, healthy and determined. He also decided to lead his team through a different starting route. Willpower and persistence pushed him through the harsh Khumbu Icefall terrain and onto a new pathway.

Edmund was part of a team who after twelve days reached South Col which is a significant staging area for a final summit push. The day was May 21 which gave them a short period of time before heavy snowfall would obstruct a summit. From the team a former president of the Oxford Mountaineering Club - Tom Bourdillon, and a brain surgeon - Charles Evans, were chosen to attempt the first summit. However at 28,700 feet they ran into oxygen problems. Exhausted both men understood that soon they would run out of oxygen and agreed to go back.

Three days passed, Edmund and local sherpa Tenzing Norgay started their attempt to reach the mountain top. Tenzing was a local Sherpa who was chosen because he had already proven his summit potential. In fact, he was the most experienced and had been at least four thousand feet higher than any of the others had. No one had gone with someone with such experience before. Tenzing had been part of six previous attempts to summit the mountain. He had the feedback and it paid off. Hillary and Tenzing reached the highest point on Earth at 11:30 a.m. on May 29.

So feedback is important. If you want to climb to the top of the mountain and reach your goals then you need some sort of feedback system in place. First of all you need your goals written down. As mentioned earlier that could be in a notepad or it could be in a document on your computer. A computer is much better because you can easily edit it and organize as you progress. But whichever you prefer.
So what does feedback on your goals involve? Fundamentally it's about checking you're on the right path and making progress. Therefore you need to be honest with yourself and question your progress. Make sure you ask the right questions to really probe into how you're doing. Ask yourself what you are doing good, what you are doing bad and what needs to change. In addition, come up with more questions relevant to each of those goals. Let's take a look at some examples.

Health

Let's say your goal is to lose 5kg and get a six pack. Your plan would probably involve some diet to be in a caloric deficit so that you're losing weight. Plus you will have some kind of exercise regime in place. Right there's a few things that you can measure. Then you could start asking yourself some of the following questions. Did I complete my exercise plan for this week? What would I rate myself out of ten this week for my exercise plan? Then you could ask yourself about your diet. Did I stick to my diet? What would I give myself out of ten this week for my diet? Those are just some example questions. You can come up with your own as you wish. Just make sure they give you some useful answers.

Going further you could ask yourself what was good about your progress? What was bad about it? What do you need to do to improve? What changes do you need to make? What habits do you need to implement? What things do you need to stop? What is standing in the way of you achieving your goals? How can you overcome it? Write your answers in a short paragraph and that can be like a summary of how you are progressing. Each month you can keep an eye on your progress and make adjustments as necessary.

Relationships

Okay so let's say that you're single and your goal is to find your ideal partner to be in a relationship with. Some of the things in your goal plan might be to go on dates, build confidence, create an online dating profile and go to two social events a week. Okay, so there are some things which you can measure. Ask yourself, did you go on any dates this week? How did they go? What went well, what went bad and what can you improve? How about your dating profile, is it attracting the right people? What's good about it, what's bad about it and what do you need to change? How about your confidence levels? What would you give them out of ten? How can you raise them? Did you go to any social activities this week? What social activities could you go to next week? Again now you'll have a good summary and understanding of where you are towards achieving your goal. You will know what you need to do to achieve it.

Finance

As an example let's assume that you want to double your income in six months. Part of your plan to double your income could be to find a new side come. You could ask for a pay rise at your job. Also you could find an investment that increases your wealth. So there you have three things that you can measure your progress by. Ask yourself some questions. What actions have you taken towards increasing your income? What questions could you ask that investigate whether you have fulfilled the objective? Have your actions been fruitful? What changes do you need to make? Have you found any side hustles? Did you ask your boss for a pay rise? Have you come up with a good set of reasons to present to your boss as to why he should raise your salary? Have you taken action on making any investments? Why not? What do you need to learn? What you need to do? The quality of your questions will determine the quality of the answers. Come up with a question that will give you a clear picture of what you need to do going forward.

How often should I review my goals?

At the start when it comes to feedback I suggest for you to review your goals every week. Do that for the first six months and then when you get a better understanding of how to review goals you can do it every couple weeks or every month. But always make sure you review them at least once a month.

Okay great, so as you can see the review can give you some key insights into how you are doing and what you need to do going forward. Without this you won't have the right feedback to be able to climb those mountains and succeed in your goals. Be sure to do that regularly and it's even better if you can get help from your peers or mentor to guide you through that process. When you have set some goals it is vital that you frequently review and assess them. This allows you the time to ensure that you're progressing in the right direction and staying relevant.

Reward yourself often

Reward yourself for your successes, but don't punish yourself for failure. before you set a goal identify why you're setting a goal. Reward yourself every single step of the way. When you achieve little tasks, set up a reward. Maybe that's a little holiday somewhere or a day off for some time to enjoy a nice movie. Just make sure that the process to what your goals is a pleasure. Celebrate your wins, even the small ones. This will keep you emotionally engaged in momentum.

<u>CONCLUSION</u>

Congratulations on completing your journey to the end of this book. Goal accomplished! I'm excited that you now have some goals that you're excited about. You've taken a powerful step with goal setting and you're on a path towards a better future.

Without those goals you would just be drifting through life. Now you have purpose.

Since we're at the end of this book I want to take a moment to summarise some of the most important topics that were covered. Allow me to refresh those in your mind. First of all we talked about what goal setting is. Goals are something that guide and focus us towards changing our life for the better. This encourages us to achieve a high level of success and become a more self actualised person.

Moving on we talked about how to actually set your goals and what your goals should be. The goal setting process outlined here has four steps. You can find an action guide for that process in the bonus chapter. In brief it is as follows. Step one is to set yourself some goals in different sections of your life and those are.

- Health. Relationships. Friends. Family. Finance. Career. Travel, Passions & Adventure. Lifestyle. Learning. Spirituality/ Mental Health. Giving

In step two you analysed your goals and set time frames for each. Those time frames were.

- 1-month. 3-months. 6-months. 1 year. 5 years. 10 years or more.

At this point you should have quite a few goals and you need to move on to step three. Organising your goals into a spreadsheet or a notebook. At this point you can start to prioritise your goals. As discussed there are some essential parts of goal setting and those are.

- Planning: You're much more likely to stick to your goals when you have a specific plan for them.
- Clarity: Having a clear vision.
- Quantification: Making it measurable.
- Enumeration: Defining tasks.
- SMART+: Make your goals fit into the SMART+ framework. That is they should be specific (S), measurable (M), achievable (A), realistic (R), timebound (T) and positive (+). The human mind is particularly sensitive to negativity and positivity. It's been proven that it's best to put your goals into the positive, present tense.
- Motivation: The gasoline, it is what will encourage you to achieve a goal.
- Time Management: Goal setting relies heavily on being able to manage your time well.
- Flexibility: Not all your plans will go as you expect. A flexible attitude is necessary
- Persistence and focus - Obstacles will also come your way. At those times you're going to need to be persistent, focused and keep moving forward.
- Challenging: Set goals that are a little bit out of your reach. This will keep you engaged.
- Self-regulation: The ability to regulate and manage your emotions.
- Vision: Paint a clear picture in your mind's eye that inspires you.
- Feedback: Track and measure your results. Do it frequently.

With our goals set we then started to look at the obstacles to achievement. Those are caused primarily by the other goals you have which compete against each other. The Four Burners Theory was introduced as a method of considering ways in which we can become more effective towards goal achievement. That means that sometimes we will have to shift the focus of our attention on to other goals and let the other goals simmer in the background. Sometimes you can put other goals in maintenance mode. Maybe for a period of time you choose to focus on one goal and let the other ones stay in maintenance. We also talked about some of the ways that you can outsource various activities to ensure that you are spending your most valuable time on the highest leverage things. All of this requires a ruthless attitude.

At this point in the book you would have some worthwhile goals to focus on. But without a plan in place you will never go anywhere. Here, the when, where and how of accomplishing goals was discussed. Productivity and habits can increase your chances of achieving your goals via a much more streamlined process. Additionally, that includes aligning your environment with your goals. The simple act of keeping a clean and tidy environment with minimal distractions is a surefire way to accomplish your goals.

Following on some further tips for setting your goals were presented. Most goals are possible to achieve but the thing that holds many people back is motivation. In the chapter on motivation we dived deep into how it affects goals. Much is the same with motivation; you will also require persistence to stay on track towards your goals. You might be talented but without persistence you will never get anywhere. In addition, surround yourself with the right people to keep you going. Those can be your mentors and peers. Furthermore you can create vision boards to form visual representations of where you're going. This all feeds your subconscious mind to bring you closer to achieving your destiny. We explored that your human mind is strongly sensitive to visual stimulation and subconscious messages that can be presented through vision boards affirmations and riding out your goals everyday. In summary there are a number of ways that you can stay motivated and those are.

- Set boundaries: Set yourself some simple boundaries that will keep you motivated because you know that there will be a break coming up.
- Break it down: Big goals need to be taken one step at a time. Stay motivated with small wins.
- Minimize distractions: Distractions will keep you from your goals. The truth is focus is not really about optimization it's more about subtraction. Remove or block any distractions.
- Education: If you feel you're not progressing fast enough just ask yourself, do I have the appropriate knowledge? Study the relevant books, enroll yourself in a course or even hire a mentor and acquire all the relevant knowledge .
- Waste no time: Start right now on your goals. Take a definitive action right away. Become motivated by your actions.
- Embrace failure: The successful realize that failure is part of the equation and it doesn't affect their motivation. It just makes them more motivated to try again and succeed at all costs. Never give up.

Great stuff there to keep you motivated! Moving on the importance of time management was introduced and shown to be an essential skill for goal setting. When you learn how to manage your time you have a much better chance of success. Become great at planning and prioritizing the time you have. Implement a system or try selecting your most important tasks for the next day. Place your activities into four different sections based on urgency and importance. Learn to say no to the things that will take away your time. In addition, cultivate a flexible attitude. Sometimes things will require a different approach. Your plans should not be so rigid that they can't move around natural obstacles and challenges. Plus you need to be open to new opportunities as they come up.

In the last chapter some of the ways that goals can be set in teams, academia and group settings were introduced. In order for team leaders and managers to be successful they need to be able to communicate the goals of their organisation to their team members. Team goals need to be in line with the individual goals of the team to create a harmoniously successful environment. This is undeniably important towards the united effort of success. Specifically the method introduced was the OKR (objectives keys and results) which is a system used by Google and various other leading companies. Through setting measurable goals it can be used to create alignment and engagement in a team. Application of OKR ensures that goals are frequently set, tracked and evaluated. This is perfect in corporate and team working environments because it really engages everyone involved. Thus making sure that everyone is headed in the same direction with clarity is a strong advantage of the method.

Finally we talked about feedback and how important it is to achieving your goals. without a feedback system in place you'll never know where you are on the pathway to your goals. Feedback can be in a notepad or on a computer. Most of all you need to be consistent with it and make sure that you're tracking your progress. Ensure that you're asking the right questions of yourself and what changes you need to make going forwards. When you reach milestone accomplishments be sure to reward yourself.

Excellent so that is a summary of this book. The truth is that achieving your goals is a journey. It's not only about the destination. Because you don't want to arrive at your goals and then be disappointed. The journey there should be enjoyable. Make sure you consider that when you set your goals.

At the start of this book I promised you that you are capable of achieving goals that go far beyond what you believe is possible. Goal setting is something that can raise the bar of your potential and push you to achieve those things that you didn't think were possible before. If you start small and get some small wins under your belt then you can raise the bar higher and higher. Before you know it you will be far away from where you imagined you could be. Make goals a part of your life and that will come true for you.

Go ahead, give it a try.

BONUS GOAL SETTING GUIDES

The Four Step Goal Setting Process

Step 1:

Divide your life into:

Health. Relationships. Friends. Family. Finance. Career. Travel, Passions & Adventure. Lifestyle. Learning. Spirituality/ Mental Health. Giving.

Brainstorm what you want in each area. No censorship, write as fast as you can. Come up with questions or use some of these prompts.

Do you want to? Feel? How? Try? What? Time? Would you like? How much? How many? Achieve?

Step 2:

Analyse your goals and set time frames for each.

1-month. 3-months. 6-months. 1 year. 5 years. 10 years or more.

Step 3:

- Enter your goals into a spreadsheet or a notebook.
- Prioritise your goals. Eliminate any that are not so important.
- Focus only on the goals that are most important to you.

Step 4:

Get SMART +
Use the S.M.A.R.T. protocol to make sure your goals are optimised.

Specific (S). Measurable (M). Achievable (A). Realistic (R). Timebound (T) and positive (+).

Make a plan

Select your goals and break them down into clearly defined steps.

- Work backwards, step by step from achieving your goal
- Brainstorm and list every action that needs to happen
- Figure out the people, resources and materials that you need
- Identify the daily, weekly or monthly habits that will move you closer
- Study the relevant books, enroll yourself in a course or even hire a mentor and acquire all the relevant knowledge .
- Set time frames and use a calendar to help you.
- Surround yourself with a team of people that will inspire you to move forward. They could come from reading biographies, YouTube videos, listening to music or in person.
- Create a vision board. Start finding pictures that represent those goals, the feelings around them and the experiences.
- Write out your goals everyday.
- Affirmations are another great way to install your goals into your goal seeking subconscious.

- <u>Start right now on your goals.</u>

Keep your plans together in some kind of planner. I recommend Google sheets and a calendar.

Thanks for Reading

What did you think of, *"Goal Setting + Morning Routine: Discover The Blueprint To Achieving Your Goals & Maximizing Your Productivity With Morning Rituals & Success Habits (2 in 1 Bundle)"*

I know you could have picked any number of books to read, but you picked this book and for that I am extremely grateful. I hope that it added at value and quality to your everyday life. If so, it would be really nice if you could share this book with your friends and family.

If you enjoyed this book and found some benefit in reading this, I'd like to hear from you and hope that you could take some time to post a review. Your feedback and support will help this author to greatly improve his writing craft for future projects and make this book even better.

I want you, the reader, to know that your review is very important and so, if you'd like to leave a review, all you have to do is click here and away you go. I wish you all the best in your future success!

Thank you and good luck

Oscar Monfort

Other Books By Oscar Monfort

Quit Your Job: How to Live Out Your Dreams, Pursue The Work You Love & Achieve Financial Freedom

Quitting isn't easy, But if you are thinking about leaving your job then keep reading before you turn in your resignation.

In a 2018 poll, over 50 percent of Americans were found to be "actively disengaged" and having a poor or miserable work experience. If you also are not happy or satisfied at work, then it's time to identify what it is that's making you so unhappy and make changes.

Whether your dream is to start a business, travel, or have more free time for yourself. It doesn't matter if you don't even have a plan yet because this book shows you how.

Take the leap into a better life, discover what you love and make your dreams come true with this book.

https://www.amazon.com/Quit-Your-Job-Achieve-Financial-ebook/dp/B082V12644

Rituals Of The Rich & Famous

Success Tips, Strategies and Habits of The Rich & Famous

Get 4 new strategies every week on how to be more productive, confident, and happy.

Get Access Now

www.ingramcontent.com/pod-product-compliance
Lightning Source LLC
Chambersburg PA
CBHW050732030426
42336CB00012B/1522